Kay Douglas has a special inter... difficulties and women's empowerment. She has work.... social worker, counsellor, group facilitator and psychotherapist for 18 years. Kay currently maintains a private therapy practice. She also works at a Women's Centre as a counsellor and a psychotherapist and as a co-facilitator of men's Living Without Violence programmes.

Kay is passionate about the importance of women's stories. Her first book, *Invisible Wounds: A Self-help Guide for Women in Destructive Relationships* (The Women's Press, 2000), has helped to empower many women who are in, or recovering from, destructive relationships.

She lives in Auckland, New Zealand with her partner and is the mother of three adult children and the stepmother of two children.

Kim McGregor has specialised in working with child and adult survivors of interpersonal violence since the mid 1980s. She is a Clinical Associate in the Psychology Department, University of Auckland, where she is completing her PhD and is also a Research Fellow in the Injury Prevention Research Centre (University of Auckland). In addition she maintains a small private therapy practice and is the author of *Warriors of Truth: Adult Survivors Healing from Childhood Sexual Abuse*.

She was born in the United Kingdom but now lives by the sea in Auckland, New Zealand with her partner and daughter.

Also by Kay Douglas from The Women's Press:

*Invisible Wounds: A Self-Help Guide for Women in
Destructive Relationships* (2000)

POWER GAMES

Confronting Hurtful Behaviour
and Transforming Our Own

KAY DOUGLAS & KIM McGREGOR

Published in Great Britain by The Women's Press Ltd, 2001
A member of the Namara Group
34 Great Sutton Street, London EC1V 0LQ
www.the-womens-press.com

First published in New Zealand by Penguin Books (NZ) Ltd, 2000

British Library Cataloguing-in-Publication Data
A catalogue record for this book is available from the British Library.

ISBN 0 7043 4474 2

Printed and bound in Great Britain by Cox & Wyman, Reading, Berkshire

Kay dedicates this book to:
My family: my partner, John Bailey; my children, Robert,
Jenny and Angela Clancy;
and my stepchildren, Hannah and Thomas Bailey.
Also to my professional families: the North Harbour Living Without
Violence Collective and the North Shore Women's Centre.
I am truly blessed by your support, encouragement, love and belief in me.

Kim dedicates this book to:
My partner, Richard Hanssens; daughter, Rachael, and son, Stephen
(passed away); family and friends in New Zealand and England –
thank you for the gifts you have given me: love, support, joy, memories.
Colleagues, mentors and clients living in many parts of the world –
thank you for sharing with me your life stories and wisdom.
Knowing each of you has enriched my life.

CONTENTS

Acknowledgements

There are many people to acknowledge in a project of this size. Most importantly a very special thank you to all the women who generously shared their hearts, experiences, wisdom and inspiration in the personal interviews for this book. Without you this book could not have been created.

We would also like to acknowledge and thank the following professionals who read parts of the manuscript and offered valuable feedback: Fay Lilian (Anger Change Trust), Lorraine Owens and Margi Keys (North Shore Women's Centre), Leslie King and Éliane Whitehouse (Phoenix House Counselling and Psychotherapy), Maggie Caitlin and Kerry Gould (Inner City Women's Group) and Sue Treanor.

Thanks also to our publishers, Kirsty Dunseath at The Women's Press in London (and at an earlier stage Kathy Gale), and Geoff Walker at Penguin New Zealand, for their ongoing commitment to this book despite the time it has taken to produce it.

Kay Douglas:

My heartfelt thanks to my partner, John, for his sustained understanding, patience and acceptance of how important this book has been to me. The equality, respect and freedom in our relationship continues to heal and nourish me. I also thank my children, Jenny, Angela and Robert, for being the supportive, generous and caring people they are.

I am grateful to my clients. They have enhanced my understanding, enriched my life and inspired me personally and professionally by sharing their struggles, hurts and triumphs with me.

My appreciation to all my friends and colleagues who have supported and encouraged me in this project, most especially Patti Turner, Andrea Clark and Jenny Lloyd for their cheerful typing assistance. A special thank you to Ruth Palmer and Gay Rowley for feedback on parts of this manuscript.

I am deeply indebted to the team at the North Harbour Living Without Violence Collective and the women at the North Shore Women's Centre. Their ongoing encouragement and affirmation of my work has helped to sustain me through the tough times. It is an honour to work with such committed and passionate people. A special acknowledgement to Catherine Johnston, whose clarity, courage, compassion and generous spirit are a shining example of personal power to me.

Kim McGregor:
I would like to acknowledge my partner, Richard. His enduring love has healed my life and has given me confidence to be in the world. I thank Richard for his contribution to the first draft of this book when I was grappling alone with the huge and unwieldy concept of power. His input into the stimulating discussions we had helped to formulate my thinking. He also read parts of the manuscript over several years of this project and gave helpful suggestions. Love and admiration go

to my daughter, Rachael, who has been a loyal and constant supporter of me throughout her lifetime.

Over the last fifteen years I have worked with survivors of inter-personal violence. Each of my clients has generously taught me about the struggles and joys of human relationships. I have drawn upon your wisdom for this book. Thank you.

I would like to thank my many friends, colleagues, and mentors for their different gifts. For their on-going support of me, special thanks go to Dr Heather McDowell, Kathryn McPhillips, Johnella Bird, Carole Beu, Debi Hart, Matthew Fitzsimons, Greg Smith, Lorraine Carryer, Jacqui Fill and colleagues at the Auckland Women's Centre, Dr Alison Towns, Dr John Read and colleagues in the Psychology Department, University of Auckland, Sara Bennett, Dr Carolyn Coggan, Dr Janet Fanslow and colleagues in the Injury Prevention Research Centre, University of Auckland.

Final thanks go to Kay. We met as touring authors in the Top 20 *Listener* Women's Book Festival in 1994 and became good friends sharing in each other's celebrations. I was sad for Kay when she became ill. I felt honoured when she asked me to step into the gap and to write the first draft of this book alone. It was a privilege to work with the courageous and inspiring words from the women who told their stories for this book and to begin to draw together a foundation for this important topic. Later I enjoyed the process as Kay and I wrote the second draft together. I felt excited as I experienced the dynamic of us sharing and melding our clinical and theoretical knowledge. Each discussion about power clarified the difficult concepts that we were attempting to describe. Each draft of the manuscript was an improve-ment on the last. Therefore, because Kay wrote the final draft alone, and added an entirely new section on parenting children, the majority of any congratulations for this book go to her.

Introduction

This book has been written for women who feel caught in power struggles, for those feeling powerless, those who worry that they are misusing their power and hurting others and those wanting to claim and express power with integrity.

When one person exerts power over another in order to get his or her own way, without due regard for that person's feelings, a power game is taking place. Power games rob us of our dignity and self respect and sap our joy in living. When used repeatedly power games can reduce the recipient to feeling incompetent, self-doubting and confused, in a word: powerless. The person misusing power may also eventually begin to suffer feelings of guilt, isolation and distress about the damage he or she is doing to important relationships.

Power games do not serve people or relationships well. Hence our desire to write a book to help women to address the issue of the hurtful power in their lives and encourage them to claim their personal power more fully. Personal power is generated from within by self-awareness, confidence and self-esteem. It is the respectful power we can use to stand up for our rights and have our say without harshly undermining others. We (the authors) believe that when we are standing in a position of personal power we are less likely to allow ourselves to be deliberately hurt and less inclined to feel the need to exert destructive power over others.

This book is designed to guide you through a process of clarifying the dynamics of the power struggles in your life, identifying the impact, reflecting on the underlying issues and making positive changes. In writing this book our goal has been to make it positive and uplifting, despite the fact that this subject can be 'heavy'. Power games and powerlessness are learned behaviours which we firmly believe can be changed if we are willing to commit to this. Above all else we wanted *Power Games* to be practical and solution focused. We have included dozens of anecdotes, insights, ideas and specific suggestions for moving away from hurtful power and finding an authentic sense of power within. At the end of many sections there are check lists or questions designed to help you to deepen your process by relating the information you have read directly to your own situation.

The information offered is influenced by our own search for empowerment, our work with individual clients, Kay's work in the living without violence field, discussions with other professionals and the women who were interviewed.

This book is divided into four parts:

Part One: Exploring the Issue of Power

Part Two: When Others Use Power Games Against Us

Part Three: When We Use Power Games Against Others

Part Four: The Journey To Personal Power

Part One is a general section intended for all readers which explores the issue of power and guides readers through a process of reflecting on their way of expressing their power. If you clearly identify yourself as either the one being hurt or the one doing the hurting it will probably be most helpful to turn next to the section that applies to you (either Part Two or Part Three). Later you may chose to read the other section to gain some understanding of the dynamics from the other person's perspective. However you will notice the book is very much about focusing on what is happening for you, rather than expending your energy analysing the other person.

Sometimes deciding which section best applies is not so clear cut. You may recognise you have a tendency to swing back and forth; sometimes being the powerless one, at other times the aggressor. In this case read both sections and gather some strategies from each.

Part Four is also a general section which applies to all readers. It contains many strategies to help women develop a sense of personal power.

Women Helping Women

Fifty-five women shared their stories for the making of this book. Some are women who have used their power destructively against others. Some were subjected to power games by their partners, parents, siblings, children, neighbours and at work. All have suffered the pain of power struggles and have taken steps towards gaining personal power. The women vary in age, backgrounds, sexual orientation, culture, financial situation and personal circumstances. Names have been changed to protect their identity.

Their stories are stories of struggle, healing and personal triumph and are a tribute to the incredible strength and determination of the women who shared them. They are individual stories, yet so much of what they have been through is part of a universal experience that highlights women's resilience and courage and ability to heal our deepest hurts and move towards realising our potential.

Many of the women commented on how power games locked them into a place of secret shame, unable to find the help they needed to change. We hope the honesty in these stories provides the impetus for other women to seek openly the support they need. Where there are people being hurt, secrecy and shame serve no-one.

Our concern in producing a book which gives a public voice to women who have hurt others is that it will be used against women. We fear that these women's honesty will be hailed as 'proof' against the feminist analysis that much of the destructive behaviour by men against women is based on men's underlying belief that they have the right to assume power over women. I (Kay) know from my work as a co-facilitator of men's Living Without Violence programmes that sexist attitudes are at the heart of many men's abuse of their partners.

When you work in this field you repeatedly hear the argument that 'women can be abusive too'. We all know this is true but this statement conveniently ignores the fact that in the vast majority of cases it is women and children who suffer at the hands of males, rather than the reverse. The implication of 'equality' that is implicit in this argument denies the reality that men are usually physically stronger than women and that they generally hold more power economically.

In our experience, women's abuse usually does not come from a position of domination, strength and entitlement as men's power games often do. Rather it more often comes from a place of rebellion against oppression, reaction against feelings of powerlessness and/or outrage and pain caused by previous abuse. The experience of women interviewed for this book who acknowledged hurting others certainly supports this belief. Many had suffered abuse that left them deeply wounded. It was from this place of wounding that much of their destructive behaviour came.

Keeping a Journal

Throughout this book you will find many questions and written exercises which are designed to assist you in understanding your relationship with power more clearly. Writing can be a powerful tool which helps us to discover our true feelings, clarify our thoughts and define our experiences. One of the interview women described what her writing meant to her:

> I believe the change in our situation has to come from inside of us. For me writing has been a vital part of my growth. I've just written and written, just allowing myself to follow the flow of my thoughts and feelings. My journal is really, really important to me. The value of writing is that the feelings are caught. I go back often and read things that I have written and that is really helpful.

When doing the written exercises allow yourself time alone, uninterrupted. Your writing is for your eyes only so keep your journal somewhere private. Don't worry about spelling, grammar, punctuation or messy writing. Just relax and allow yourself to express your deepest feelings and thoughts uncensored.

Consider Finding a Support Person

Although obviously it is possible to work through this book alone we would like to encourage you to find a support person to work with. A support person can be your guide if you feel lost, your encourager if you feel hopeless and your solid rock if you are confused. She or he can offer you honest feedback and a reality check if you become confused. One woman clearly captured what her support person meant to her:

> When I decided to change my sister helped me to get all the feelings out. To be able to voice whatever I was feeling. Those things are really hard. Sometimes I'd get a bit frightened to say how I felt because I'd think that that person is going to think I'm stupid and what's coming out of my mouth isn't making any sense, but she allowed me to work through it until I came to the other side.

Rather than asking the person to be there solely for your support you may decide to buddy up with someone who also wants to work at increasing her personal power and agree to support each other. It can be affirming and empowering to compare notes, share insights, set small goals for change together and debrief after trying out new behaviour.

When choosing a support person it may be helpful to ask yourself:

◗ Will this person stand by me and offer positive, supportive input?

◗ Do I trust this person?

◗ Has she or he proved trustworthy in the past?

◗ Will this person respect my confidentiality?

Having decided on a support person you will need to let her or him know exactly what you are trying to achieve and what kind of support you might require. You may want them to provide a listening ear, help you to plan and rehearse new behaviours or challenge you if you begin to lose sight of your goals. The clearer you are, the more likely you are to get the kind of support you need. Obviously you will need to be aware of your support person's limits and be careful not to put unrealistic demands on her or him.

The Birth of this Book

Power Games was conceived six years ago. The journey has been long and the gestation and birthing process challenging. Yet it has been a labour of love, for the subject is dear to our hearts. We know from our own experience how soul destroying hurtful power can be, not only for the one on the receiving end but also for the one doing the hurting.

Because of my own personal struggles with issues of power I (Kay) was delighted when the publisher approached me to write this book. I rearranged my busy timetable, naively assuming it would be close to completion within the year. It is perhaps fortunate that I never dreamed that it would take so long to finish this book – nor that it would be such a challenging process.

I decided at the outset to interview women who had experienced hurtful power struggles and to allow their experiences to bring this book to life. The interviews proved to be heart rending, humbling and inspiring. I was progressing well when I began to develop occupational overuse syndrome (OOS) through using the computer. I kept going slowly, with care, but gradually the precious time I had put aside for this book began to slip away and other commitments began to crowd in. Eventually, 18 months after I had begun, I approached Kim to work on it with me.

Since then the challenge of doing justice to a subject so important and complex, our busy schedules and my OOS have made progress painfully slow. At times it has seemed doubtful this book would ever be completed, but our desire to produce a book that would inspire women to step out of power games and claim their personal power has thankfully won out.

Our hope is that this book will help you to become more powerful in the very best sense of the word – to speak out, live boldly and make a difference.

As you work your way through this book go at your own pace, attempt the strategies that feel right for you and most of all be kind to yourself along the way. Remember to celebrate your efforts as well as your successes.

We wish you well.

PART ONE

EXPLORING THE ISSUE OF POWER

CHAPTER 1

Women and Power

P ower is an active force which we use to influence one another and express what is important to us. We all want to have our needs met and feel in control of ourselves and our lives. We all want a degree of power in our relationships with other people: to assert ourselves, to be listened to, to be taken seriously, to have our opinions respected and to feel confident. In our day-to-day life our power is constantly called into play when we are required to say no to others' demands, stand up for ourselves, speak our truth and make ourselves heard. In some situations we may cope well but in other settings we may feel powerless and silenced.

Although power is a reality of life it is an issue many women struggle with. As much as we want to have power in our dealings with others we may also feel ambivalent about it. We know from experience that power can be overwhelming, intimidating, intoxicating and harmful. We can use our power to hurt or help, control or encourage, diminish or uplift one another.

We have probably all experienced the agitated, anxious feeling of being on the end of someone else's destructive power: the shock of being treated unfairly, the stinging humiliation, maybe the outrage and fear, and all too often the helplessness. Likewise we have probably all experienced the momentary surge of strength and triumph when we have got our own way by imposing our power over someone else, perhaps followed by guilt and remorse. Most of us are also familiar with a quieter, more confident sense of personal power that enables us to voice our concerns, stand our ground on issues that matter to us and express our opinions directly, yet respectfully.

Our sense of power obviously varies enormously with the circumstances we find ourselves in. In some settings we may feel confident and safe enough to be outspoken, while in others we shrink into the shadows. When we feel vulnerable we may withdraw into silence, yet when our passion is fired we become forthright and fearless. When we feel angry or hurt we may lash out destructively to bring someone down.

Most of us are faced every day with situations that require decisive action. Our two-year-old throws a tantrum, our supervisor demands we work late when we have another engagement, our teenager is hassling to go to a late-night party, our neighbour wants us to baby-sit yet again, our partner puts us down . . . In each of these dilemmas we may respond with hostility, assertiveness or passivity. In any given situation we can choose to slip into powerlessness, to express our power destructively, or to express it honourably. The choices we habitually make in these everyday situations will gradually shape our relationships and our lives, as well as affecting the lives of those around us. Gradually our choices will lead us towards or away from true empowerment.

This chapter explores the issue of power in women's lives. It defines and contrasts the use of hurtful and respectful power: power games and personal power. It also explores the issues of powerlessness and the power imbalances and conflict that can be a feature of particular relationships. Throughout this chapter women speak about their experiences with power.

Power Games: The Hurtful Use of Power

Power games can be defined as the destructive use of power by one person over another. We are involved in a power game when we use our power to undermine someone for our own ends. Power games are about control, winners and losers, scoring points and gaining the upper hand at the other's expense. One woman offered the following description of being on the receiving end of power games:

> *Keith treated me like I didn't exist most of the time. He wouldn't even look at me for days on end. If other people were around he'd pretend things were okay but he'd roll his eyes upwards when I spoke, or address me in a really patronising way, or snigger or smile mockingly when I spoke, as if I was stupid.*

Power games as a means of gaining control may be blatant or very subtle.

> *I knew I shouldn't be so hard on the kids but it seemed the easiest thing to do. It was a quick fix. Give them a hiding, put them to bed and they'd shut up for a couple of hours. Smacking with the wooden spoon was often enough. Often I'd smack on the leg, pull their hair, clutch them hard, privately in church for instance. That was something I hated in myself, that silent bullying.*

We are using power games when we:
- try to make others feel guilty so we can get our own way;
- refuse to listen to their point of view, speak down or ridicule;
- bully someone into agreeing to our demands;
- deliberately confuse someone by distorting the facts, denying the truth or telling lies;

- intimidate someone by becoming overbearing and angry;
- discriminate against someone on the basis of their race, sexual orientation, age, disability or for any other reason;
- 'push someone's buttons' to get the response we want;
- abuse someone by name-calling, putdowns, harsh criticism or threats.

We may use our power destructively in a conscious way or we may act hurtfully with little awareness.

> *Power-tripping was something that I did without a second thought. I thought it was normal behaviour. I'd seen it with my parents. It's always been that I'm the only person that I can rely on, so I thought I had to be selfish and aggressive because I was the only one who would look after me. I was always using power games but I never even considered how it affected the other person. Each time a relationship broke up I'd think, 'Oh well, that's what happens,' and that was that.*

Using power games may force quick compliance but this may be short-lived. People will often capitulate if we put enough pressure on them, but when the moment of influence is past they may well rebel, particularly as they are likely to be feeling hurt and resentful. This means that we often need to become increasingly overpowering to maintain control. This of course takes a toll on the relationship and leaves the person on the receiving end feeling increasingly worthless. Naturally they withdraw to protect themselves from further hurt.

It is the relentlessly undermining nature of power games that often makes them so damaging. Over time the recipient's self-esteem and sense of personal power may be stripped away completely.

> *I became a total wreck in the end. I couldn't understand why this was happening. I was crying all the time, I lost my confidence, I*

felt totally worthless. I kept having time off work because I was
worried sick about what to do.

Often the impact on the person inflicting the pain can also become
increasingly destructive.

I felt like shit. I was riddled with guilt every time I abused someone.
My life wasn't worth living, I hated myself.

We can easily feel downtrodden and insignificant if someone is
constantly getting the better of us. For some of us that will trigger a
sense of helplessness that immobilises us. Others respond by standing
their ground and taking steps to protect themselves, while others
resort to using destructive power themselves in retaliation.

Questions to Consider:

▶ How often do you find yourself on the receiving end of
someone's destructive power?

▶ What impact does this have on you?

▶ How often do you express your power in negative ways?

▶ Who do you exert this power over?

▶ When you use power games what is the impact on yourself
and the people around you?

▶ Which role are you most frequently in: the one doing the
hurting or the one being hurt?

▶ Is this an established pattern that is causing problems for
yourself and/or those around you?

▶ Would you like to make any changes?

Personal Power: The Respectful Use of Power

Personal power is power that is characterised by integrity, sensitivity and
respect towards ourselves and other people. Personal power involves
honouring ourselves and honestly speaking our own truth. Personal

power is about self-control, co-operation, equality and clear communication. One woman defined personal power in this way:

> *Personal power for me is when I stand tall, know who I am and*
> *speak my honest truth. Being true to myself and integral with*
> *who I am, but not in a way that hurts other people. Like saying,*
> *'This is who I am and these are my limits. I'm not having abuse in*
> *my life', and at the same time not behaving in ways that hurt other*
> *people either. I find myself in this place more and more now. It's a*
> *place of inner strength where I feel centred and sure of myself.*

We are expressing personal power when we:

◗ set the ground rules for our child and stick to them;
◗ say no to our supervisor when we don't want to work overtime;
◗ insist our doctor refer us to a specialist for a second opinion
   when we have doubts;
◗ refuse to listen to our partner's or parent's harsh criticism;
◗ challenge someone who is being racist;
◗ make a complaint if we are being sexually harassed at work;
◗ use our personal experience as a basis for political action.

Personal power is the type of power displayed by Mother Teresa and
Mahatma Gandhi – the power to influence others in a positive way.
Through their respectful behaviour toward others they gained trust
and loyalty and continue to influence and inspire us even after death.

It is clear that power games and personal power are very different
types of power. Both influence other people, but in very different ways.
When we use power games we may get our own way but we also
disempower and alienate others, destroy trust and engender fear and
loss of confidence. In contrast, when we relate from a place of personal
power we maintain our integrity and the dignity of ourselves as well
as the other person. We are also more likely to create co-operation,

closeness and honesty, build trust and engender confidence in others.

Questions to Consider

▶ With what particular people are you able to express your personal power?

▶ What makes this possible?

▶ When you are acting from a place of personal power how do you express yourself?

▶ In what areas of your life do you find it difficult to express your personal power?

▶ Why is this?

▶ What would it take to increase your sense of personal power?

Powerlessness

To feel powerless is to feel vulnerable, alone, unsure, discouraged, overshadowed, impotent and fearful. When we feel powerless we are likely to become apologetic, compliant and passive; afraid to express our thoughts and feelings in case we offend, displease or invite confrontation. We compare ourselves unfavourably with others. The other person seems powerful and threatening and this may in fact be so. We perceive ourselves as fragile, helpless and inadequate.

It is natural to begin to feel powerless if we are being persistently undermined by someone. Ongoing power games are likely to erode the confidence of the strongest of us over time.

This woman was experiencing power games at work. She graphically describes her sense of powerlessness:

> *I was like a little mouse in a maze, going round and round in circles. When things happened I couldn't see my way out. I was constantly doing this hesitant questioning of myself and by the time I worked out what was happening and realised I was innocent it was too late. I began to feel I couldn't do the job. They got me*

worked up into such a pitch it was just, 'Yes, Ma'am, I'll do it.' I
was under so much pressure I'd panic and just file things every-
where just to get rid of them. I bitterly regret that in the end I
compromised my own standards. I should have just said, 'I'm
sorry, I can't clear all that at the moment.'

Many women in particular struggle to overcome a pervasive sense of powerlessness. This is not surprising considering our long history of being disempowered in our patriarchal society. Although there have been some changes, many of us continue to struggle with issues of self-esteem. The sense of entitlement and belief in ourselves that would enable us to claim and express our power boldly can be elusive and fleeting.

We may also have personal issues that contribute to our feeling powerless. One woman who has a history of abuse described how an ongoing sense of powerlessness continues to overshadow her life:

I find it hard to cope at work. Even when I feel strongly about an
issue and I want to speak out I just can't bring myself to. I'm
scared that I'll make a fool of myself. I don't want the spotlight on
me. Maybe I'm wrong and other people will think I'm stupid.
Maybe they'll get mad at me if I come up against them. I don't
want any hassles so I keep my mouth shut. It's easier that way.
But I do end up feeling stewed up and angry at myself sometimes.

We are behaving powerlessly when we:
- avoid conflict and confrontation at all costs;
- allow others to sway our opinions or make our decisions for us;
- accept other people's criticism whether it is justified or not;
- allow ourselves to be interrupted or dismissed when we are speaking;

▶ try harder and harder to please someone who is hurting us;
▶ fail to take appropriate action to protect ourselves from
    another person's abuse.

When we feel powerless we are inclined to forget that we have choices.
Doubtful of our ability to hold our own, we would rather avoid the
possibility of conflict than take the risk of speaking out for what we
believe. In choosing to remain silent we may maintain a level of
emotional safety but we usually pay a price for this, with dwindling
confidence and self-respect and a growing sense of shame. As we
shrink away from expressing our opinions and making our needs
known our lives become narrower and more restricted. Feelings of
resentment, frustration and helplessness can create tension, headaches, depression, anxiety and other health problems.

Questions to Consider

▶ In what situations do you feel most powerless?
▶ Why is this? What are you afraid of at these times?
▶ What makes you lose your sense of power?
▶ Are there people in your life who you feel disempowered by?
▶ How does this happen?
▶ How do you act towards others when you feel powerless?
▶ Are there changes you would like to make?

When Powerlessness Leads to Power Games

Sometimes when the pressure becomes too great we may switch from
being passive and powerless to using power games ourselves to help us
regain a sense of control or discharge our pent-up emotions. As we
assert our will over someone else we gain an increased sense of power.
We can believe, at least momentarily, that we are superior, strong and
in charge.

Sometimes rather than risking a blow-up by expressing our anger directly we may look for another outlet to relieve our angry feelings and regain a sense of power. This is called displacement. One woman shared her experience of this:

> *My bullying was very much fuelled by anger. If I'd had a bad weekend at home, Mondays and Tuesdays I was really bad. I'd just go out and provoke and dump on people. It was just misdirected anger. At the time it made me think I had some control and I liked that feeling, but the anger wasn't directed at the people that it should have been directed at and so didn't solve anything.*

If we are looking to take our frustration out on someone else we are likely to choose someone we see as less powerful than ourselves. Sometimes children become the target.

> *The more my partner was abusive, the more I'd turn on my son. It was like I'd lost control in our relationship but I had control of him. My partner was controlling me but I could control my son and getting some control made me feel more powerful.*

Although we may try to compensate for feelings of powerlessness by resorting to power games, feelings of power gained in this way are likely to be fleeting. Real power is not gained by using control tactics over another. *Real power is gained by being true to ourselves, living by our principles and acting in ways that are respectful of ourselves and other people.*

When Power Games are One-sided

It is a common myth that 'it takes two to tango'. This translates to: when there is conflict it takes two people to create it. This is not true. When power games are being played there is usually one person who is committed to having his or her way regardless of the impact on the other. In many situations the other person is preoccupied with how to stop the conflict and will often make all kinds of attempts to do so, from confrontation to peacemaking to capitulation, all the time hoping the bullying will stop.

If the power games continue, both parties usually get locked into a pattern. The person doing the hurting becomes increasingly aggressive and committed to the controlling behaviour, while the other becomes worn down from trying harder and harder to please, in an attempt to avoid the hurtful episodes.

As strange as it may sound, both parties in this situation need to gain more personal power. The person doing the hurting needs to move away from the destructive use of power and learn to use his or her power with integrity and sensitivity in ways that are respectful of the other person's rights and needs. (See Chapter 12 'Choosing to Change' for a discussion of strategies.)

The person on the receiving end of the hurting obviously needs to increase his or her sense of personal power: to find ways to care for, strengthen, protect and stand up for themselves and communicate their needs if appropriate. (See Chapter 7 'Becoming More Powerful' for a discussion of strategies for this.)

Questions to Consider

▶ In your interactions with others do you think you tend more towards powerlessness, power games or personal power?

▶ Generally are you able to express yourself honestly and openly? If not, what stops you?

▶ When there is conflict how do you go about dealing with this?

▶ When you feel frustrated, resentful or angry towards another person how do you express this?

▶ How do you feel about the way you express your power?

▶ Would you like to make any changes?

▶ If so, how would you like to change?

When Power Games are Two-sided

Occasional clashes and conflicts between people are inevitable. However, we are becoming embroiled in two-sided power games when both sides are so intent on 'winning' they no longer care how they wound each other. If we are being hurt by another's bullying, fighting back with power games ourselves can seem to be the only alternative to being crushed.

I was determined to give as good as I got. I'd been hurt before so I wasn't going to put up with being brought down without a fight.

But fighting back agressively comes at a cost. As two people use power destructively against each other the relationship can degenerate into a painful game of tit-for-tat payback that leaves both parties feeling increasingly emotionally battered.

When we are caught in constant conflict and both parties are using hurtful behaviour it can be difficult to define who is responsible for what. As women we are socialised to take responsibility for relationship difficulties, so we may readily blame ourselves for the conflict. Even when women resort to lashing out in an attempt at self-defence they often end up believing they are the guilty party.

There is a big difference between taking responsibility for our own hurtful behaviour and becoming over-responsible and taking on the blame for someone else's. While taking responsibility for our own destructive behaviour is a vital step towards change, taking the responsibility (and blame) for the other person's behaviour is inappropriate and counterproductive.

To gain some clarity about the underlying dynamics within your conflicted situation reflect on the following questions.

Questions to Consider:

▶ Who has the final say on most issues of conflict? *IMT*

▶ Which person's needs, wants and opinions are given the most importance and are most often catered to? *IMT*

▶ Who does most of the giving and who does most of the taking in this relationship? *I give, he takes (emotionally)*

▶ Who has the most power in terms of decision-making and control over the finances and other resources? *IMT*

▶ Do you most often find yourself in the role of 'winner' or 'loser' at the end of arguments? *Loser*

▶ Who is the most fearful? *Me*

▶ Is your hurtful behaviour an attempt at self-defence? *Yes*

▶ Are you trying to retaliate for the other person's hurtful behaviour? *Yes*

▶ Whose mental/emotional/physical health is suffering the most? *Mine*

▶ Are you afraid for your physical safety? *No*

▶ What insights have you gained from these questions? *How far I've submitted.*

Our History as Women Doesn't Help Us to Be Powerful

Many women are uncomfortable with claiming and expressing their power fully. The social stigma against powerful women who may be often referred to as 'cold', 'selfish' or 'hard bitches' can make us fearful of inviting criticism. Most women have also had distressing experiences of being on the receiving end of harsh power tactics and this adds to their uncertainty and anxiety. One woman clearly captured her ambivalence:

> I've got two conflicting parts of me. One is terrified of power
> because I think that when human beings use power it can be the
> most destructive force on earth. My family have used that
> immense power over me in the past. The other part of me would

like to have power to be honest and truthful and say what I think in a way that might help other people. This is a different use of power. There's a part of me that's terrified that if ever I personally had power I'd become destructive. I'd love to have the positive power, to be honest and say the truth. I'd like to have the power that is like a light that gives other people strength and courage. But I'm absolutely terrified of having power and hurting someone. That's my greatest fear, that I'd purposely use it to hurt or destroy someone. I'd never want to do that.

Historically women have had few models of female power to draw from, since women's acts of courage and power have largely been missing from the history books. Small wonder we often don't fully recognise, claim or embrace the power that we do have.

Many of us have been brought up in a patriarchal style of family, where father was the head of the household. Adults had the say and children were expected to be seen and not heard. In this traditional family (many of which are still around today) the man's word had ultimate power.

My father had that quiet, cold anger and that was more frightening than if he'd shouted and screamed. I knew the moment he was in the house. All I can remember is never being able to do things without being jumped on. Before he got home the little kids would all be bathed and clean, we were fed, the table was cleared and the dishes done, the kitchen was spotless. Everything had to be perfect when he walked in the door. Intimidation was what kept it all going. Everything revolved around Dad, our whole lives, our emotional well-being, when we ate, when we slept, when we used the bathroom.

Some would say times have changed – yet there are many women who still live in fear of incurring the wrath of a domineering partner.

As committed as we may be to gaining equality, many of us are held back not only by our circumstances but by a lack of belief in our right to claim our personal power. In times of stress or conflict we can find ourselves slipping into the peacemaker role and keeping others happy, just as we have been socialised to do.

This is not surprising. For centuries our power as women has been undermined. Historically society prescribed a role of powerlessness, compliance and obedience for women. This was reinforced by laws that ensured women were legally under the authority of their husbands and had fewer rights than men. Unable to gain power in their own right, women were usually restricted to gaining a sense of power through the status and wealth generated by their husband's place in the world.

The dogged determination and collective action of the women's movement has brought about an increase in status, human rights and autonomy for women in recent years. Thankfully women in western society nowadays have more freedom to pursue their own careers and interests and to make decisions about their own lives. Yet there is still a long way to go before true equality exists.

Traditional beliefs and attitudes about women being less important than men are still alive and well. In many settings, women are still expected to sacrifice themselves and their needs to serve others in the name of duty. Many men still believe their ideas and opinions are more valid and their needs more important than those of the women around them, in the workplace as well as in the home.

Obviously these attitudes have an impact on women's self-image and sense of power in the world. Because these beliefs are part of the fabric of our society women as well as men are influenced by them. This helps to explain why we can sometimes be so hard on ourselves and other women who we perceive as not conforming to society's 'rules' for women.

Power games don't just happen because we experience the destructive use of power within our families or because individuals hold sexist attitudes and beliefs. The traditional family is a reflection of our patriarchal capitalist world in which certain people are privileged because of their gender, race and wealth. Our society is founded on a win-or-lose dynamic. In the competition for financial and material resources there are clearly those who emerge triumphant and those who remain at the bottom of the heap, trapped hopelessly in the cycle of economic powerlessness.

The Journey to Personal Power

With all the many changes that have taken place we continue to grow and redefine what it means to be a woman. We continue to find ways to stand up for what we believe and to claim the autonomy that is rightfully ours. Claiming personal power is about allowing ourselves to have a full and passionate life in which we boldly overcome obstacles in our lives and gain increasing strength, clarity and personal freedom. This is achieved by learning to listen to our inner knowing, clarifying what is truly important and honouring this by action.

At a practical level the many choices we make to be true to ourselves help to build our sense of personal power. Each time we use our power with integrity to stand up for our own or others' rights in a respectful way we are enhancing our personal power. In this way our confidence gradually builds and our self-esteem blossoms. As we increasingly experience ourselves as powerful women who are entitled to be treated fairly it becomes easier to find the courage to challenge those who would put us down.

While each of us can practise expressing our power more fully at an individual level we also need to be aware that our power as women is encouraged or impeded by the amount of respect given to women in our particular society. The challenges of strong women have brought about changes in women's status in Western society. Just as these women have paved the way for us to live more powerfully we too can pave the way for other women by challenging oppression, discrimination and inequality. One of our greatest strengths as women is our ability to be creative and nurturing, to show compassion and to act collectively.

Reaching a place of personal power is a journey of growth that can be a huge challenge, especially if our previous experiences with power have been destructive. While on this journey we need to be gentle with ourselves, to create strong support along the way and to allow ourselves to take small steps. The many small acts of power we perform are the footsteps on a journey that will be ongoing as we develop our skills and potential and tackle the challenges life presents. Although it may be daunting at times, becoming more personally powerful is also freeing and exhilarating, as the women in this book testify.

> *Claiming my power has been a real journey. I feel right now as if I'm on the top of a mountain. It's felt like I've walked miles over really hard, stony roads with bare feet and it's been painful, but I'm finding it a little bit easier now and I'm beginning to see how far I've come and it's really exciting. I'm still working on setting boundaries, building confidence and trying new things and that's okay. I've come a long way. I feel as if I'm getting somewhere. Now I'm finding I can laugh more easily. I'm able to be myself. I can let my humour and my being come out without any fear of reprisal. I'm really so pleased to be at this new place. I never want to be where I was before. I've found me.*

This chapter has defined and explored the issues of hurtful and respectful power: power games and personal power. You may have recognised you are caught in a pattern of power games, either as the one on the receiving end or the one doing the hurting, and need to make some changes. If so we suggest you turn next to the section which best applies to you: Part Two (When Others Use Power Games Against Us), Part Three (When We Use Power Games Against Others), and use this as a guide on a journey to personal power.

PART TWO

WHEN OTHERS USE POWER GAMES AGAINST US

CHAPTER 2

Being Hurt in Close Relationships

I s there anything more heartbreaking than being hurt by a person we are close to? Although others may also hurt us we are usually more deeply wounded by those closest to us – our partner, parents, siblings, children or close friends – because whether we like it or not they matter. These people know us and our history and as such they have enormous power in our lives.

Those close to us are supposed to support and comfort us in times of trouble and celebrate our special moments with us. Yet for some of us this affirmation, love and encouragement is not forthcoming. Sadly, those we are close to can bring us the most grief when they choose to use their power to wound us with insensitive criticism, control us with their demands, shrivel us with their indifference or attack us with harsh words or actions.

If we are being hurt by someone we are close to we are likely to struggle to make sense of what is happening. We may feel intensely emotionally attached, yet in a way that hurts. When we see others having happy connections with their loved ones it can rub salt into the wound because it reminds us of what is possible and what we don't have. Our head may tell us to stay safe by keeping our distance, yet our heart longs for closeness, appreciation and reassurance of our worth. Disappointment, resentment and helplessness can bind us tightly to the hurtful person. We may love them, yet at times hate them.

This chapter explores the various uses of destructive power within close relationships through the experiences of women who have lived the pain. Hurtful behaviour can take many forms, as the following stories show.

Guilt-tripping

I feel overpowered by my sister. She's always borrowing money off me and expecting to help herself to anything in my house she wants. She goes from crisis to crisis and phones me in the middle of the night expecting me to be there and listen and pick up the pieces. If I ever try to stand up for myself she gets angry and tells me that it's not fair, I've always been Mum's favourite, I'm the one with the good job and she's got nothing. I only think about myself. Or she'll break down and cry and tell me I don't care about her. Then I feel really awful, like I'm being mean to her and I should try harder.

People who use power games are usually committed to getting what they want. Somehow their needs and desires are more pressing, greater and more important than ours. This person may play on our sympathy or use guilt trips to pressure us into 'helping' them. But behind the supposed 'helplessness' of this person there is often a strong determination to have us meet their needs. We are expected to listen, encourage, comfort, rescue and solve their problems. Unfortunately the more we give, the more the other person tends to expect. If we try to say no or suggest the other person takes care of their own problems, increasing pressure is often brought to bear. We may be reminded of how important our help is and how much the other person is suffering. We have the power to make their situation 'better' and if we are a 'good' person we will do this. If not we are accused of being self-centred and to blame for the other person's suffering.

> I've been left looking after my father since Mum died and it's hell. He doesn't seem to realise I have a life too. He expects me to be there all the time and to wait on him hand and foot. He's always going on at me: 'Where have you been? I thought you'd be here hours ago. I'm sitting here all on my own but you couldn't care less. You've always been a selfish bitch. After all I've done for you. You just want to get rid of me. You'd like to see me in a home. That would suit you. I don't know what your mother would say about you if she was here.' There's just no pleasing him.

Criticism and Control

> Brian wanted to take charge of everything. Everything had to be done his way. If I cooked a meal and didn't do it the way he thought I should he'd go on at me. He'd criticise my driving, the way I answered the phone, the way I hung washing on the line. If I drove to the shops he'd get really furious if I didn't take the route he thought I should. He was always watching me and if I didn't do as I was told I was reprimanded like a naughty child and he'd fume for hours.

Sometimes a person close to us assumes the right to control our actions, decisions and freedom. Everyone has different ideas, beliefs, priorities, habits, preferences and responses to the world around them. People who use power games often find it difficult to accept these differences. They have little if any room for compromise or flexibility. They see differences in terms of 'right' and 'wrong' – and their way is 'right'.

Giving with a Hidden Agenda

> *My mother's always offering to help me but then she throws it all back in my face. She phones me about five times a day and offers to clean my house or do my washing or lend me money. Sometimes I feel as if I'm suffocating. When I tell her I don't need her help she gets really angry: 'I don't know what's wrong with you. You won't let me do anything to help you. You're not like other daughters. You've got a nasty streak in you. I don't know what I've ever done wrong that you won't accept my help.' It's really awful. I just want to get on with my own life but I feel as if I can't.*

Excessive giving can be a form of control that keeps us in a 'one down' position. When someone insists on helping, advising, problem-solving, pulling strings and making our decisions for us, while overriding our protests, our power is undermined. Of course not all giving is bad. But when it is accompanied by emotional manipulation and a lack of respect for our real needs and boundaries it becomes destructive. Gifts and favours can be enticing but accepting this form of 'help' from someone wishing to control us can put us under obligation and this can be used against us. In this situation our efforts to set limits and live our own lives often meet with huge resistance and sometimes punitive attacks that leave us feeling hurt and guilty. We are placed in a painful emotional bind where we either feel bad for resisting the help or bad for letting ourselves down by taking it.

Put-downs

> *My husband would often make derogatory remarks about my colour and race – even after I told him I found it hurtful. When I first came to this country there were lots of things I didn't know and I didn't understand. Everything was different, our way of clothing, food, bedding. It felt like I didn't exist any more as a*

person. It was so distressing. If I asked for anything to be explained my husband would make a joke out of it. Instead of explaining he'd say something derogatory, usually in front of people. Also if I pronounced a word wrong he'd bring this up in public and tell everyone, but sometimes nobody even laughed and sometimes they even felt embarrassed for me. His way of making himself 'one up' was to put me down. He could say whatever he wanted to say. As long as I didn't open my mouth that was fine. The minute I opened my mouth I was accused of washing dirty linen in public. I wasn't allowed to say a word. It was very shaming and belittling.

Our loved ones know us well, so their opinion matters. They have the power to champion, support and uplift us. Unfortunately when this special power is used to undermine and put down the impact can be devastating.

Sulking and Withdrawing

John would refuse to talk to me or even look at me for days but when we were around other people it would be a different story. He'd pretend everything was normal and be all attentive and even make jokes with me. Then as soon as we were on our own he'd go back to refusing to have anything to do with me. He just wanted everyone to think he was a great guy. And they did!

The silent treatment can be a powerful tactic used to manipulate us into compliance or punish us for non-compliance. Most of us find it distressing being around someone who is refusing to acknowledge us. If sulking is accompanied by smouldering, silent anger we are likely to feel on edge and perhaps frightened. Our attempts to break the ice and discuss the problems may be met with further withdrawal or a sudden outburst of anger.

Communication Games

> *If I ever want to talk about something my son laughs in my face, or turns the music up loud, or blocks his ears, or runs off. I see these ways of dismissing any communication as a form of bullying because he is determining how we relate. I have no control over it at all. Even if I say, 'Good morning', he cuts it off: 'Leave me alone. What do you want? I'm rushing off.' It is manipulative behaviour. He's keeping the power.*

Honest, clear and kind communication builds and strengthens relationships. A person misusing power usually does not want to explore the issues openly or take responsibility for their behaviour. Instead they use tactics that confuse, disempower, sidetrack or derail us. A smoke-screen of blame and accusations may be created when we attempt to discuss issues of concern. The person may deny the truth, tell lies, bait us by becoming hurtful or offensive, distract us by changing the focus of the conversation or overpower us by refusing to let us have our say. These games often leave us feeling bewildered and impotent.

> *When I wanted to communicate I ended up waiting for three weeks until my partner was in the right mood before I could actually sit down to talk, and even then it was, 'What do you want?' in a really nasty voice. It made me feel really frustrated and eventually I just gave up. I tried to say I wasn't happy but it was always twisted back on me. It was my fault – I wasn't understanding enough, I nagged too much, I didn't allow enough space. It was always me.*

Possessiveness and Jealousy

> *I became really isolated when I was with Jan. I had a lot of friends before the relationship but she seemed really threatened by that.*

She used to give me such a hard time when I spent time with them. When I got home she'd stand over me and go on and on badgering me about where I'd been. If I wanted to invite people over she'd get all moody and tell me she wanted to spend time alone with me. If we did see friends she'd totally withdraw and afterwards she'd spend ages saying all these nasty things about them. After a while I gave up seeing my friends. It just wasn't worth the hassle. I figured I was better off at home with her. It saved a lot of fights.

A person may use power games to keep us to him or herself. There are many ways of making contact with other people uncomfortable. Criticising our friends and family or picking fights with them, making us the brunt of hurtful 'jokes' or putting us down publicly are a few. After a while it can seem easier and safer to shun social contact. Unfortunately as we become isolated from friends and family we become less sure of ourselves and more dependent on the hurtful person to meet our needs and affirm our worth.

Sexual Control

Keith was always putting the hard word on me for sex. If he didn't get what he wanted he'd get really angry and storm around the house slamming doors and making sarcastic comments, or else he'd sulk for hours. Often he'd just hassle me and threaten to go somewhere else until I gave in. It was constant pressure. When we did have sex I was never doing it right anyway, according to him.

Our bodies are our own and we have the right to decide if, when and how we want them touched – even within the context of an intimate relationship. Sexual control is occurring when one person is pressured into sexual involvement that they don't want. Undermining can take many forms, including cutting sexual comments and comparisons that make us feel put down or worthless. Threats to 'go elsewhere' can be made or demands for sex 'as of right'. Barbed comments about sex (or the lack of it) and hurtful jokes can be used to cause embarrassment. Sulking, withholding affection and angry outbursts can be used to manipulate us into complying with sexual demands, or to punish us if we resist. We can also be intimidated or forced into sexual practices against our will.

Using Money to Maintain Control

Jim is forever questioning me about money, wanting me to account for everything and accusing me of being extravagant when really I'm just the opposite. If I buy anything for myself or the kids he gets sulky and makes all these pointed comments about business being bad and how hard he works and I end up feeling guilty. Yet if he wants something for himself it's not a problem. There always seems to be money for his interests, no matter how much they cost.

Control of money represents power – and can be a useful tool for maintaining the upper hand. Within an intimate relationship finances can be used to gain power by controlling joint money, withholding money for necessities, blaming us for expenditure and using double standards that allow our partner to have the pleasures that money can buy while we do not.

Bullying the Children

Every night at the tea table there'd be a scene. Gavin always wanted the meal on the table at 6 o'clock. The kids and I would be sitting around the table and we'd start to talk about the day and what had been happening and the next thing we'd hear him coming down the path and the silence would be profound. Before he came up the first step he'd start to pick on someone to put their bike

away. Then it would be: 'Sit straight at the table,' or 'Eat properly.'
He'd find seven or eight things to yell about. These dear little kids
were just sitting eating their dinner and no-one was allowed to
speak. It was just constant tension.

Some women find themselves in a position of unsuccessfully trying to protect their children from their partner's bullying. As mothers we are often well aware of the way our children suffer in the hands of an overly controlling parent or step-parent. Even if they are not being abused directly, children are usually deeply distressed when they see or hear other people being hurt. They feel powerless and impotent at not being able to protect their loved one and may even blame themselves for causing the abuse. When there is emotional or physical abuse each family member will adapt and try to cope in their own way.

Chris was really hard on my children. He picked on my son
constantly and isolated him out of the family. And my son coped
by rebelling. He actually ran away from home when he was 10
after a blow-up over a stupid little thing. It was so awful. He
eventually left home at the age of 16, but I know he had some
really bad times before that. I always used to feel as if I was
sandwiched between Chris and my son. My terrible regret now is
that I was really weak. My daughter says she can only remember
me as a shadowy figure in the background. I was so overwhelmed
with my own feelings, I guess I just didn't really address what was
happening for my children. My daughter says she decided that her
brother was getting such a hard time that the only way she was
going to get in Chris's good books was by being very good and very
compliant. So she became very quiet and withdrawn, only talked
when she was spoken to.

Our children rely on us for protection. If we honestly consider they are being harmed it is vital that we take action to keep them safe.

Chapter 7 'Becoming More Powerful' contains many suggestions of ways to confront the power games in our lives.

Sometimes it is impossible to protect children while living in the same house as the person who is doing the hurting. If we have tried unsuccessfully to discuss the problems and get that person to take responsibility and seek help to make the necessary changes it is then we need seriously to consider separation. Many women eventually leave abusive partners because they are unable to protect their children and in hindsight they often wish they had left sooner. (For further discussion on children see Chapter 14 'Parenting With Personal Power'.)

Angry Outbursts

> *My father kept right on giving me a hard time and treating me like a child when I got married. He was always telling me what to do and if I didn't do it he'd start shouting and calling me a stupid bitch in front of my husband and children. I put up with it for years and would try to talk to him and put my side of the picture and convince him that what I was doing was okay, but it never worked out. It only kept the argument going because he just wouldn't listen.*

Most of us find it distressing to be around someone who has angry outbursts. Wanting to avoid conflict we often allow ourselves to be manipulated into compliance. If that person resorts to breaking possessions and making threats this can become terrifying. We are being made very aware that from that point it is only a small step to personal physical violence.

Intimidation and Violence

> *My 23-year-old son is really verbally abusive towards me. He threatens me and has done things like slapping out at me, pushing me against the wall and waving a knife at me. Just a couple of*

weeks ago he said, 'If you don't shut up I'll hit you over the head with a baseball bat.' It was chilling because he was just sitting there in front of a friend and there was no emotion attached to the words, so I had no way of interpreting whether he was just being smart or whether he meant it. That night I was fearful about going to sleep by myself. I thought, 'Shall I take the dog into my bedroom for protection?'

Physical abuse is not just hitting and punching, it includes behaviours such as restraining, shoving, kicking, shaking, spitting, pushing, slapping and hair-pulling. Once begun, physical abuse usually develops into an ongoing pattern that escalates in severity and frequency. *Physical violence towards another is totally unacceptable. There is never any excuse that justifies this behaviour.*

Once my husband had hit me that was it: I was frightened. He's not a big guy, but when he did it I was absolutely amazed at the power that was behind it. I just couldn't believe that he could hurt that much. It was a real shock. He didn't hit me every night, but it happened maybe 10 times and that was 10 times too many. It really lowered my self-esteem. Before that I used to think, 'How come these battered wives just stick around?' I always thought that if anyone ever hit me I'd hit them right back, but it just wasn't like that.

Many women who are being threatened or are suffering physical assault fail to recognise the seriousness of the situation at the time. If you are being hurt physically it is vital to realise you are in danger and to seek protection. (See 'Keep Yourself Safe', p. 132 and 'Community Resources', p. 272.)

Exercise: Name the Power Games

An important first step in overcoming the power games in our lives is to clearly identify the other person's hurtful behaviour for what it is, at least to yourself. Without a clear perspective on what is happening our power is limited. When we stand back from the hurtful situation, clearly identify that we are being treated inappropriately and acknowledge that this is not acceptable we are in a better position to protect ourselves and deal with the situation.

> *Looking back I think a major turning point came when I finally recognised that what my partner was doing to me wasn't okay, it was abusive. She was always giving me a hard time, constantly putting me down and harassing me when I didn't do what she wanted. It took me a long time to figure out that it was her bullying behaviour that was the problem, not whether or not I lived up to what she wanted.*

To clarify your own experience in a difficult personal relationship complete the following list by checking (✔) each statement you clearly identify with and putting a question mark (?) beside those statements that are true for you some of the time.

_____ I am being put down, criticised, belittled and/or undermined by someone close to me.

_____ This person uses the silent treatment to punish or manipulate me.

_____ I feel I am being taken advantage of.

_____ This person often refuses to respect my 'no'.

_____ The relationship with this person feels oppressive.

_____ This person puts pressure on me to sacrifice my needs in order to meet his or her needs.

_____ This person refuses to listen to my point of view.

_____ I am being isolated from other people and/or undermined in my close relationship.

_____ I am being coerced into doing things I am not comfortable with.

_____ This person often blames me and tells me I'm wrong.

_____ This person often emotionally manipulates me by using guilt trips and/or playing on my sympathy or my sense of obligation.

_____ I cannot discuss the behaviours I am upset about openly with the person concerned.

_____ This person pretends to be respectful in front of others, then hurts me when no-one else is around.

_____ My freedom, choices and actions are often being controlled.

_____ The hurtful behaviour is becoming more frequent and/or destructive.

_____ I am frightened by standover tactics, angry outbursts, threats and/or the other person smashing things.

_____ I have been physically abused in some way (including pushing, shaking, slapping, kicking or punching).

If you have acknowledged that some of these power games are being used against you by someone close you may be feeling quite shaky. When we face the truth about a hurtful close relationship we often experience very mixed emotions. We may feel sad, angry or shocked. We may be afraid that if we come out of denial and face the difficulties squarely it will threaten the relationship. We may also be relieved that we now have a way of making sense of our experience. All these feelings, however conflicting, are an important part of your journey. Allow yourself the time to feel your feelings. Express and work through them by talking to your support person or writing in your journal. It is important that you take good care of yourself at this time.

It *is* possible to regain your power, so be encouraged, and read on. One woman offered the following hard-won advice to women readers who are still going through it:

Deal with the situation as soon as possible. Before this happened

I'd be a lot more tolerant, to the point of letting things get into mountains instead of tackling them while they were still molehills. This situation has taught me a lot. It has been a really hard time and I hope I never have to repeat it, but it's been a real rebirth time as well. What it has made me do is to stand up for myself and react a lot more quickly. It's taught me that I need to get in earlier, rather than ignoring it and hoping it will go away, because it doesn't, not with something like power games. It just gets worse.

CHAPTER 3

Being Hurt in the Workplace

Hurtful power games in the workplace can have a profound effect on our emotions and health. Although work is only one aspect of our lives, for many of us it is an important one. When we are appreciated for doing a good job and treated with respect work can enhance our self-esteem and confidence. The opposite is true when a supervisor, employer, colleague or subordinate begins to undermine us.

Women are particularly vulnerable to power games in the workplace, frequently suffering attacks on their dignity, negative stereotyping, discrimination and harassment in various forms. Without a doubt some people do give women a hard time in the workplace, simply because of their gender. Those outside the mainstream in terms of race, ethnicity, sexual orientation, religion, social class, age, disability and health are often also the targets of others' destructive power. At times we may be undermined out of jealousy because the person recognises and resents the fact that we are more competent, skilled or popular than them.

Some power games are so blatant that we are left in no doubt as to their injustice. More often they begin insidiously with veiled put-downs, subtle control tactics, unfair criticism and sarcastic comments that leave us increasingly confused. Our strengths, skills and intelligence may be devalued. We may be subtly singled out and made an example of or accused of under-performance. Rather than clearly identifying these as power games we may be inclined to take on the blame or give the person the benefit of the doubt.

If this pattern continues to escalate we are likely to find the problems increasingly playing on our mind and overshadowing other areas of our lives. Our heart sinks as we contemplate another day at work. We worry about what to do and mentally rehearse clever answers for 'next time'. But when the time comes we often find ourselves too afraid to risk speaking out.

Most of us don't want to engage in destructive conflict in the workplace. Conflict takes time and energy, which are often in short supply for women juggling their busy lives. Most of us depend on our income. If we fight back we often fear jeopardising our job, especially if the power games are being played by a supervisor or employer. These people hold a degree of legitimate authority, so we are not on an equal playing field. Although this authority certainly does not give the person the right to treat us disrespectfully, it is likely to make it more difficult for us to challenge and overcome their hurtful power.

This chapter explores some of the many forms of power games played in the workplace.

Constant Undermining

I can only describe what happened in my job as mental cruelty. It was so subtle. How do you tell people about the innuendoes, the sneering looks? I just don't know where to start. My boss would harass me, wouldn't let me do my work. He'd talk to me and hold

*me up, he'd bait me, he'd pick on me to upset me. He was very
moody and changeable. I never knew what to expect. He'd set me
three or four really difficult jobs and he'd want them all done at
once. It was deliberate, so that whichever one I did he'd be hassling
me to get the other ones done. He'd have me going in three or four
different directions at once. After a while I started to lose my
confidence. It was the beginning of horrendous bullying.*

Sometimes it can be hard to put our finger on exactly why we are feeling inadequate and disempowered because the attacks may be so subtle. We may be ignored, treated in an offhand manner, sniped at, whispered about, set up so that we appear incompetent, deliberately passed up for promotion or have our ideas stolen or discarded. Alternatively we can be criticised and hounded in very obvious ways. Unrealistic expectations can set us up for failure. There are many ways to create no-win situations so that when we predictably fail the person playing power games has an excuse to berate us.

*Whenever anything was wrong in the office I got the blame for it.
There weren't many things that I did right – the way I wrote
letters, the way I talked, everything I was. They were just chipping
away at me until I didn't know who I was. Eventually the boss
stopped speaking to me at all. I'd get back from lunch every
Thursday and there'd be a letter sitting on my desk. One said: 'I'm
the manager and you'll do everything I tell you.' Another was a
new job description. One day there was a letter full of criticisms
about me. That really shocked me.*

If your employer or supervisor has a genuine grievance about your performance, it should be conveyed in a respectful way. He or she has a responsibility to offer constructive criticism by letting you know specifically what the particular issues are and how you might go about addressing them.

Erratic Behaviour

The manager was so unpredictable. Sometimes he'd come up and push past me and almost knock me flat. Sometimes he'd say, 'Good morning,' and make a real fuss and the next time he'd just stand there and glare at me silently and then take off and almost flatten me. It was so nerve-wracking. I never knew what to expect.

Working with an inconsistent person who is sometimes pleasant and at other times hostile and aggressive is likely to leave us feeling constantly on edge.

My workmate was so moody. I never knew where I was. Sometimes she'd be as nice as pie, then she'd get really snappy or wouldn't even speak to me. A few times she got in a real temper and shouted at me for things I didn't even do. I used to get really uptight just being around her. It really got me down.

Acting in a Two-faced Way

The worst part of being bullied was not being believed. Don had a very plausible manner and he spoke to the public quite gently. There were never any witnesses to what was going on. We were always in the office alone when it happened. Eventually I went and talked to the boss and he said, 'I don't believe it. Don wouldn't do that.' It was Don's word against mine and that's the way it always stayed. He was so plausible and gentle-mannered to everyone else, you would never have picked it. That's why people wouldn't believe me. I always looked like the bad one.

It is not uncommon for the person playing power games to present as perfectly charming in public and then to become aggressive in private where there are no witnesses. The person being bullied is then likely to have a lonely uphill battle gaining support.

Intimidation

> *My boss would constantly try to force me into compliance. My job*
> *wasn't permanent and he'd say, 'If you don't do this then I'm not*
> *going to recommend you for the permanent position which is due*
> *to come up.' As a single woman I couldn't afford to lose my job but*
> *it was really in jeopardy because he was blackmailing me with it.*
> *He made frequent references to a hearing difficulty I had which*
> *wasn't affecting my work and indicated that he could use this*
> *against me if he chose.*

Power games are about retaining the upper hand. Some people who
play power games are well aware of the destructive impact of their
actions. They consciously use whatever means are at their disposal to
overpower. Others manipulatively act out their unconscious desire for
power.

> *My boss had this way of rattling off a few commands and then*
> *she'd be off, but she never gave me enough information to go on.*
> *She'd leave the main instruction out, then she'd turn her back and*
> *be unavailable. If I asked, she'd be so sharp and cutting I'd end up*
> *thinking, 'Should I ask? Am I just dumb?' and sit there panicking,*
> *flicking pages and pretending. It was her tone that was so under-*
> *mining. It made me feel small. At first I thought it was all me, then*
> *someone else came to work there and I saw her doing exactly the*
> *same thing to her. She just seemed to have this need to keep the*
> *other person off balance and to have power – to make the other*
> *person feel smaller and less in control than her. The strange thing*
> *was she seemed genuinely unconscious of what she was doing.*
> *She'd often say things like, 'I'm such a giving person. I can't under-*
> *stand why people treat me like they do.'*

Pressure to Sacrifice Health

I got occupational overuse syndrome from using a keyboard and I had so many hassles at work. I was in a lot of pain and I was supposed to be on light duties but the women I worked with didn't seem to believe there was anything wrong with me. They were always calling me 'madam' and moaning about the fact that I couldn't do things and making sarcastic little digs. Sometimes they'd just ask me to type things up anyway, even though they knew I wasn't supposed to. That would really put me in a bind because I knew if I did it I'd pay the price with my pain levels and if I didn't they'd get shitty at me.

As women we are renowned for battling on regardless when we are sick – often continuing to meet others' needs and fulfil our responsibilities at the expense of our own health. Generally this is what is expected of women. Stories about men who collapse in a heap when they are sick while women battle on are common. When a woman fails to sacrifice herself to these norms, social sanctions may be applied in the form of bullying behaviour.

Homophobia

I became aware that my boss was discriminating against women. He said, 'There's no way I will ever hire any more women. I'm surrounded by women.' I asked him to call me Ms and he said, 'Any woman who calls herself that doesn't know what sex she is. Ms is rubbish!' He went on and on about how I was very feminist. In fact I was a very low-key feminist, I just wanted to be treated with respect. If I went and got a haircut he'd give me the most disgusting looks. Even with all of that it still didn't dawn on me that a lot of what he was doing was because I was a lesbian. The day this was pointed out I was shocked! So shocked I could hardly stand

*and walk out of the office. I just couldn't believe that people could
do that.*

Lesbian women and gay men are often marginalised in the workplace and may bear the brunt of homophobic attitudes and attacks.
Lesbians are also often on the receiving end of the backlash against
feminism, especially by those who feel threatened by feminism and
assume that all lesbians are feminists.

Ruthless Competition

*I was bullied by this 23-year-old woman at work. I knew there was
something going on and that she didn't like me but I couldn't put
my finger on exactly what was happening. Eventually I rang up
an older woman in head office and she said, 'It's obvious. Angela
is out the front, painted and pretty, saying "love me, please" and
you're there, plain and ordinary and middle-aged, working your
butt off. You'd better realise that painted, pretty and saying "love
me, please" will win every time.' And that was the situation in a
nutshell. She had to get rid of me so she could be superior. I viewed
that as an emotional insecurity and felt sorry for her but in time
she set everyone against me.*

Ideally women are our friends and allies: our fellow travellers.
However, sometimes women are our harshest critics and judges. They
may knowingly undermine us, jealously compare us with themselves,
ruthlessly compete, attack our successes and be openly hostile towards
us. Some younger women can also openly subscribe to societal beliefs
that older women have less value and therefore deserve little respect.

Boundary Invasions

*Looking back I can see it was after I left my marriage that my boss
started to make a target of me and to erode me. He'd ask me about*

*my personal life, what I did on the weekends, who I was with,
where I went, what I did, how long that took, when I got back. I
thought it was funny asking me things like that.*

Sometimes someone in the workplace may appear to have an
unhealthy interest in our personal lives. Initial inappropriate questions can serve to warn us that we need to be firm and assertive about
the boundaries between work and the rest of our lives. We have the
right to our privacy. Our feelings of discomfort can act as a signal that
our boundaries are being pushed or tested and that we need to set our
limits more firmly. (See 'Become More Assertive', p. 129.)

Sexual Harassment

*I went to work in a restaurant and after a couple of days the head
chef started to come on to me. At first it was just checking me out
by asking me lots of personal questions. Then he started to make
embarrassing sexual innuendoes and implied that he wanted to
have sex with me. He was married and anyway there was no way
I would have wanted a relationship with him and I tried to make it
clear I wasn't interested, without being insulting. But it didn't end
there. One night he came on to me in the storeroom. I was really
shocked and upset and told him in no uncertain terms to leave me
alone. Two days later the restaurant owner called me in and told
me I was fired. This guy had told him I was too slow, making too
many mistakes and was offhand to customers.*

Sexual harassment is unwanted, unwelcome, uninvited and
unreciprocated sexual attention, which may be verbal or physical
in nature. Sexual harassment in the workplace can take many
forms: leering; offensive comments; intrusive or suggestive questions or remarks about one's appearance or body, sex life or private
life; repeated invitations after previous refusals; requesting sex in

exchange for special favours or a job and/or deliberate touching of any kind.

Employers have a responsibility for their own behaviour and that of their employees. Being subjected to sexual harassment, especially by someone in a position of authority, is likely to leave us feeling vulnerable, ashamed and intimidated. Sexual harassment is illegal. It is important to seek appropriate help. (See 'Strategies for Dealing with Sexual Harassment', p. 136 and 'Community Resources', p. 272.)

Racism

> I've always had trouble getting work. I'm either over-qualified, under-qualified, too young, too old – never the right age, never the right education. I did a real estate course and I went to get a job and the manager said yes – but nothing came of it so I said to him, 'This is a really nice place and I'd like to work here but I'm wondering what would it be like with the rest of your staff. Would they have any problems with me being a black woman?' And he said, 'Oh yes, I've really been concerned about that. I think they would have some problems.' I knew it was him who had the problem, not the staff! Why bang my head against the wall? Women have to work twice as hard to get into a workplace where men are dominant, and being a black woman I have to work even harder. I have to be three times as good.

Women from any and every walk of life can be, and are, harassed, bullied and discriminated against in the workplace. However, those from minority groups are subjected not only to trivialising sexist behaviour from others – these women also come up against additional prejudices and discrimination which reflect people's racist attitudes.

Discrimination against Women with Disabilities

Because I'm disabled in a wheelchair people think I'm stupid and my brain doesn't work. That's a situation that happens quite a bit. You are treated differently. It was a nightmare getting a job. I went for over a hundred job interviews. It got to the stage where I was being deceitful to get into job interviews. They would ask on the phone about health and I'd say, 'Excellent,' and that got me an interview. I knew it was discrimination I was up against because I was competing against other people I'd trained with who had fewer qualifications. I felt really down in the beginning but I realised that the only way to get a job was to keep trying. Someone was going to have to give me a job eventually.

Women with disabilities often experience problems being accepted into the workforce. They may have to contend with people's negative stereotyping and be expected to prove themselves far in excess of what is required of an 'able-bodied' person.

Being Ganged-up On

All the women ganged up and I was on the outside. I'd go in to work and say good morning to everyone and I would get no answer. No-one would acknowledge me. Total rejection! These women would all sit together and deliberately leave me out and I'd stand out like a sore thumb. I felt so embarrassed. I felt like everything was my fault. I was apologising all the time. They said it was my fault so I believed them. It must be me. It was a living hell.

Group bullying can be a particularly powerful way to bring someone down. Being talked about and/or 'sent to Coventry' by the group can cause us to feel humiliated and ashamed.

Power and Privilege

> *When I worked in the hospital what I noticed was the way the doctors related to the nurses. There was a lot of controlling behaviour and they were very dictatorial. The doctors didn't include the nurses who held valuable knowledge in discussions about work when they should have. They held on to their knowledge and excluded the nurses quite rudely. A nurse might offer some information about the patient's condition and instead of accepting and acknowledging that it was relevant, they'd say that it wasn't relevant or would indicate that the nurses didn't know what they were talking about. Then there would be the put-downs, the language – 'I know best', 'You don't know anything', 'You can't do anything right' – and the ridicule, the way that it was packaged. One doctor was particularly bad at bullying. Often what he was saying was untrue but the manner in which it was directed had such an expert power base behind it that he could have said anything and the nurses would have believed him.*

Some jobs carry with them a degree of power and privilege. Privilege is primarily associated with having high social status, professional knowledge and wealth, being white, male, able-bodied, heterosexual and healthy. The power gained through having privilege can be used in constructive respectful ways. Unfortunately privilege is also open to abuse when people view themselves as superior and insist on retaining power by treating us as less important and credible than themselves.

Exercise: Take Stock of Workplace Power Games

Obviously workplace power games happen in a variety of ways. The following list provides a summary of some of them. To clarify your experience check (✔) each statement you agree with and put a question mark (?) beside those you partially identify with.

_____ I'm often being treated disrespectfully by someone at work.

_____ There are elements of competition and/or professional jealousy that threaten my position or well-being at work.

_____ I'm being pushed relentlessly to meet standards that are set impossibly high.

_____ I'm being undermined by back-stabbing, innuendo, rumours, derogatory looks or harsh manner or tone of voice.

_____ I'm sometimes/often belittled, called names and/or criticised in destructive ways.

_____ I'm accused unfairly of things I have not done.

_____ My worries about power games at work are overshadowing other aspects of my life.

_____ I'm sometimes put in the position of looking incompetent because of behind-the-scenes power games.

_____ My personal boundaries are being violated by inappropriate questions and/or actions.

_____ I sometimes/often feel reluctant to express my opinion or stand up for what I want because I'm afraid of being put down.

_____ I am often upset by the changeable, moody behaviour of someone at work.

_____ I am frightened of losing my job because of power games.

_____ I believe I am being set up to fail and then being blamed for it.

_____ Someone at work often flies into a sudden temper and directs it at me.

_____ I am being harassed because of my age, health, race or sexual orientation.

_____ The hurtful person hides his/her destructive behaviour by pretending to be respectful when others are present.

____ I am being ganged up on.

____ I am being sexually harassed at work.

This chapter has highlighted some of the ways power can be used to undermine us in the workplace. If you are unfortunate enough to be on the receiving end of this kind of destructive behaviour, take heart. Many strategies are offered in Chapter 7 'Becoming More Powerful' that will help you begin to address your situation.

CHAPTER 4

Being Hurt in the Community

S ince our society is founded on competition it stands to reason that power games are rife in our community. On top of this, women have a long history of oppression. Who among us could say we have never been on the receiving end of power games? Most women have had many experiences of being subjected to indignities and injustice. We have become so used to many of them, we barely notice that they are insidious ways of placing us in a 'one down' position.

When construction workers whistle and shout obscenities and tradesmen overcharge us because they think we are easy prey, we may shrug these things off and put them down to experience. Aggressive drivers, hostile bureaucrats or intimidating neighbours can be more difficult to contend with, since they directly threaten our well-being. Even our personal safety is potentially at risk because of the frequent physical attacks against women. When we are alone – whether we are out in the world or even at home – we need to be cautious. We enjoy a solitary walk in an isolated place at our own peril.

We ourselves can also be guilty of wounding others through our prejudices and thoughtless or deliberate misuse of power. We can feel threatened by people who appear 'different' and can marginalise or condemn these people out of ignorance or fear. The challenge is for us to be aware of our fears and prejudices and to learn to honour and celebrate the diversity and difference of others.

Harassment of Women without a Male Partner

I had problems with my oldest son after his father left. He seemed to consider himself the man of the house and if he didn't want to do something he'd just point blank refuse. I had two neighbours who were screaming and swearing at me and telling me how useless I was as a mother and asking why I didn't do something for my son. It was just utter bedlam. I was at the end of my tether and felt really angry because I had four other kids and they didn't need to hear people swearing and being abusive to their mother, they needed to see people helping. I was always very conscious of the other four and what they were having to cope with. They'd seen their father and older brother being abusive to me and now these neighbours were doing the same thing.

People will sometimes dump on women without a male partner in ways they wouldn't if there was a man around. Women parenting alone are often discriminated against and stigmatised by society. They are held responsible for many of society's problems: the breakdown of the nuclear family, high juvenile crime rates, kids living on the streets – you name it. When children are misbehaving or acting out, 'the mother' is often directly or indirectly blamed.

Parenting alone demands constant dedication and sacrifice and the levels of stress and exhaustion can be enormous. If there have been earlier experiences of abuse by the father, it is often the mother who bears the brunt of children's resulting destructive and disturbed behaviour. She usually takes the ultimate responsibility for attempting to break the cycle. This is a formidable task that deserves far greater recognition and support. This woman's story clearly illustrates the ways that prejudices feed abusive behaviour.

> I have huge problems with both my neighbours. I think the crux of the whole thing is that I'm a solo mother. The bullying started the day I moved in. I was sitting in the car and one of my neighbours came and stood over me. He was shouting because the removal van had knocked over one of his pot plants. From then on there was trouble. He shouted at me about all sorts of things. One day I got a playhouse delivered for my daughter. His wife came over and started shouting in my face that I was a slut. I had a team of four guys there to help and she just kept screaming at me: 'So many men!' It was totally embarrassing. Then I heard from a girlfriend that they were telling everyone I was a prostitute. That really sickened me. They watched me constantly and I had to adjust to this intimidation. In the end I felt I couldn't go outside comfortably. If they see me outside they just stare at me. I try to ignore them as best I can but it has been quite devastating at times.

Neighbours who act aggressively can cause considerable distress. It can be impossible to get away from harassment by someone who lives close to us, so we can feel trapped in our own homes. In desperation some people go through the upheaval and inconvenience of moving house, avoiding certain places or leaving the community to avoid contact.

Bullying of Disabled People

> I have a type of muscular dystrophy. There was no parking near where I worked. There was parking further down the road but you had to walk back up the hill and I couldn't, so I used to park

right outside work. One day when I was parking the shopkeeper came out and said, 'Don't park your car in front of my shop. It's in the way and it's bad for my business.' She was really quite nasty and horrible about it. I went into work and burst into tears. After that it was always a problem. She was always waiting for me and she'd come out to see where I parked in the morning. She was quite intimidating. The only way I could get into work was to park outside and one of the girls at work used to move my car. It was a hassle, it really was. At times I just felt I might as well give up. It's hard enough going to work. I didn't need that kind of stress.

Women with disabilities face very real challenges. They must deal not only with their health issues and the business of living in a world that frequently doesn't cater to their needs, they are also prime candidates for power games.

Racial Discrimination

I've had lots of distressing experiences of racism. When I go into the shops the shop assistants sometimes won't serve me. One time I asked to see a figurine I wanted to buy and the woman wouldn't take it out of the cabinet because she said it was too expensive. She assumed I couldn't afford it because of the colour of my skin. Why would I be asking for something if I couldn't afford it? Could she see in my pocket? Could she look into my bank balance? I felt really very angry and insulted and belittled.

Racism is occurring when one person attributes negative characteristics to another because of their ethnicity and treats them as inferior on this basis. Many indigenous women and women of colour experience persistent racism in the community.

Religious Pressure

> *My church put me through the mill when I tried to set limits on my husband's abusive behaviour and eventually left him. When my husband was violent the elders helped me leave the house but their intention was that we be reconciled and I realised later that unless that happened they weren't going to be satisfied. Later I said, 'No, he's not changing. There's no going back. It's gone too far.' When I told the pastor he accused me of using the church deliberately. He said that I never had any intention of going back all that time. He said, 'If you don't change your mind you'll come under the discipline of the church and if you don't accept what we're saying we will have to ask you to leave.' I was absolutely devastated.*

Power can be used destructively within a religious framework when rules and regulations are imposed without due regard for our individual needs, wishes and safety.

Professional Abuse

> *I had a very nasty experience with my solicitor. I was going through a marriage break-up and he seemed really kind and caring so when he phoned and invited me out I was really pleased. At first it went really well. We were seeing each other all the time and it seemed reassuring having him work for me when I knew he really cared about me. Then things started to go wrong. I decided it was all getting too much and I wanted to back off a bit and he became nasty and started really hassling me, phoning me at all hours and giving me a hard time. The worst part was when he started to throw my story back in my face and make comments like, 'No wonder your husband left you. You've got big problems.' That was really destructive because it reinforced everything my husband*

used to say. It really knocked my confidence around and put me off
men for a long time.

There is a built-in power imbalance between a professional and a
client which needs to be respected at all times. But sometimes
professionals such as lawyers and doctors use the power and authority
of their position to their own advantage. They are privy to personal
information about us and they are in a position of trust. It is up to
them to behave appropriately and to work within the ethical standards
set by their professional body.

It is inappropriate for a professional relationship to develop into a
romantic or sexual relationship. The professional has an obligation to
act in the client's best interests, keep to their role and not overstep the
mark. He or she is responsible for maintaining appropriate boundaries
at all times, regardless of whether or not a client wants to become
romantically or sexually involved. Professional sexual abuse is
surrounded by secrecy and women experiencing it are often too
ashamed and fearful to speak out, but seeking help is vital in this
situation.

Overpowering in Groups

The philosophy of our group is that everyone has a voice and
decisions are made jointly, but in reality there is one woman who
wields a lot of power. She likes to have things her own way and gets
really impatient at meetings when things are discussed. If a
decision is made she disagrees with she gets really furious. People
tend to do what she wants because if you go against her she has
her ways of making life difficult.

Power games often happen within a group setting. This can be
particularly distressing when a group has been set up to work on a
consensus model and aspire to particular ideals of equality and

sharing of power. Even when groups are committed to a co-operative model of functioning this can be derailed by a person or people who insist on using the more traditional, competitive way of operating. Sometimes people set out to challenge oppression yet use 'power over' tactics to achieve their aims.

> When I was training, one group within our class intimidated the rest of us. They used to call us 'oppressors' and 'capitalists'. Many of us were solo parents struggling against the odds ourselves. If any of us dared to express an opinion or ask a question that was politically incorrect by their standards we were rounded on in no uncertain terms. Most of us were scared to stand up and speak. In the classroom I usually felt a mixture of anxiety, bewilderment, anger and fear. I was always questioning myself and feeling guilty but as time went on the guilt mainly came from the fact that I was too scared to speak my truth. Much of what we were learning was good, true and informative but that was tainted by my resentment at the tactics in the classroom. By the time I finished the course I often felt sick at the thought of going into the classroom. I wasn't able to stand up and speak confidently in any group, and I certainly wasn't the only one.

It is not uncommon for individuals to be swept into a category by others and labelled in a negative way in this process. This can be destructive because it can allow us to act aggressively. When people are depersonalised by being labelled negatively, for example as 'do-gooders' or 'Bible-bashers', it is easy to lose sight of the fact that they are people of worth with diverse individual beliefs.

Questions to Consider

As these stories show, power games in the community can take many forms. They often go unnamed as power games and therefore get lost in our general perception that 'this is the way the world is'. By clearly identifying bullying behaviour we are in a far better position to do something about it.

Questions to Consider:
- Which of your experiences of hurtful power in the community have left a lasting impression on you? Why is this? What did you learn from these incidents?
- Have you been hurt or discriminated against because of your race, ethnicity, sexual orientation, gender, religion, social class, age, disability or poor health?
- What impact has this had on you?
- What particular negative stereotypes are you aware of holding against certain people on the basis of their race, ethnicity, sexual orientation, gender, religion, social class, age, disability or poor health?
- In what ways does this get translated into action?
- Are you willing to move beyond the limits of your prejudices and find ways to connect with the real person instead?
- If so how will you do this?

This chapter has taken a look at the kinds of power games that are commonly played in the community. As women most of us are no strangers to the power games that are such a common feature of our society. The next chapter identifies the impact that ongoing power games can have on us.

CHAPTER 5

The Impact of Power Games

I f we are repeatedly hurt by power games it is almost inevitable that we are changed by this experience. The effects we may be painfully aware of include: shrinking confidence and growing anxiety, sadness, hurt, smouldering resentment and an increasing sense of powerlessness. We may not be fully aware of the loss of our laughter, creativity, openness, dreams, optimism, feelings of content-ment and emotional safety. These changes often creep in without our noticing amid our confusion and distress.

Of all the complex effects that power games can have on us perhaps the most profound is that we usually end up feeling bad about ourselves. One reason for this is that the person wielding hurtful power is likely to be giving us the message (directly or indirectly) that we are not good enough, a failure, guilty, over-sensitive, wrong, stupid, worthless and maybe even crazy. If these things are stated or implied repeatedly it is almost inevitable that we will begin to doubt ourselves. We lose sight of the fact that the overpowering person's behaviour is inappropriate and harmful, and focus instead on our self as somehow being the one at fault.

Ongoing power games can be incredibly exhausting. We are constantly faced with either fighting for our rights or giving in. Under this relentless pressure many of us will begin to choose the path of least resistance. In fact we may be afraid to do otherwise. In order to keep the peace and avoid conflict we may gradually start to ignore hurtful comments, give in to unfair demands and go along with things we feel uncomfortable with. While this can seem to be the best choice at the time, it comes at a price. When we repeatedly compromise our integrity we lose self-respect and feel increasingly powerless.

A destructive cycle is set up whereby we interpret our shaky sense of self, declining self-esteem, intense emotional reactions and the ways we have changed to accommodate and cope with the power games as evidence of our personal inadequacies. What we don't realise is that these responses are not signs of inadequacy – they are a natural, normal reaction to being on the receiving end of hurtful power.

Faced with ongoing power games we are likely to change in many ways. The stress of the power games, coupled with our own self-judgement, can take a high toll on our mental, emotional, physical and spiritual well-being, as the stories in this chapter illustrate.

Trying to 'Get It Right'

I was working my butt off trying to get the work through. I stayed back late, I went in early. I did my best but I still wasn't good enough. All the time I was thinking, 'I'm not going quick enough. What can I do to go faster? Where can I get that extra half hour from?' The slightest little thing and I'd feel like I was in the can again. It got to the stage that I had no confidence to do the job any more. It seemed nothing I was doing was right. Absolutely nothing. And I just couldn't take it.

Under pressure from someone who is bullying, many of us resort to trying to make the situation better by pleasing that person, hoping that if we can keep them happy we are less likely to come under attack. Women often push themselves to the brink of exhaustion trying to win the approval of a person who refuses to give them encouragement or validate their efforts.

Keeping Our Guard Up

It was like I edited everything I said. Even when I had major worries I just kept them to myself and pretended everything was fine and gave really vague answers to any questions, tried to keep the attention off me. I felt tense all the time and did my best to keep my distance. I didn't want the negativity, the free advice or the criticisms. I just wanted to be left alone.

Many of us shut down as a way of protecting ourselves from the onslaught of power games. We distance ourselves emotionally, while continuing to go through the motions of superficial relating. Inevitably we are left with an increasingly empty relationship with no real closeness. Often we withdraw not only from the hurtful person but from other people we are close to. This isolation and loss of voice adds to our sense of helplessness. We desperately need other people to provide support during this time.

I started to worry about what other people were saying about me. I was afraid that they thought I was stupid and I couldn't do my job and were talking about me behind my back. I began to feel as though I didn't have any workmates who would stand by me.

Giving Up the Things We Love

I used to have a really full-on life – lots of friends and interests. I'd

go out dancing and tramping and play sports. I used to have lots
of energy and was always on the go. Gradually that's just all
slipped away. I've almost forgotten what it's like to have fun.

As we become increasingly worn down and controlled we often
begin to restrict our lives in all kinds of ways in an attempt to keep the
peace, conserve our dwindling energy and hide our difficulties from
the outside world. We may give up contact with friends and family,
hobbies and jobs we enjoy and activities that give us pleasure.

Losing Our Sense of Self

I thought of myself as a strong, capable woman but over time all
of that got eroded. In the end I didn't know what I thought or what
I felt or what was right for me. I couldn't even make a simple
decision about what to wear to work. It was like I just didn't have
any confidence. I was just a screwed-up mess. My thinking was
so muddled. I'd change my mind and doubt everything I said.
Maybe that wasn't how it was; maybe I didn't really think that;
maybe I was just exaggerating. I didn't really know what I thought
and felt.

Ongoing power games whittle away the opinions, values, wants and
dreams that guide our behaviour and define our unique self. If we
continue to give way under pressure and compromise our integrity we
feel increasingly out of touch with who we really are and what is right
for us. As our stress levels rise we often lose concentration and clarity;
our thoughts may become scattered and our emotions intense. Many
women become concerned about their responses. Some fear they are
beginning to lose their sanity. If the person who is misusing his or her
power is also accusing us of 'going crazy' then naturally this will feed
our fears.

These symptoms are very common among women suffering in

power games. Once the ongoing stress of our situation improves these symptoms usually quickly improve.

Avoiding Facing the Problem

Living with bullying made me very fastidious. I tried to make my world as perfect as possible so I went overboard. The activity was an escape because there was nothing else to do. It was a way of not going mad. I took to arranging the house beautifully, having starched tablecloths and tea-towels, doing floral arrangements and embroidery, I learnt to knit and crochet, all those sorts of things. That was a way of coping. I didn't have to talk to anybody doing that.

There are all sorts of ways we can attempt to ease the inner pain and anxiety caused by others' destructive behaviour, including over-working, overeating and using alcohol and drugs.

Feeling Helpless

A lot of the time I felt like I was five again and I thought, 'This is not fair. I don't know what to do.' I felt like a child walking around in this adult world, just absolutely powerless. I often thought, 'I'm worth nothing,' because I felt like nothing. And then there was the intelligent adult me, and that adult was capable of loving and flowering in the desert and of being really productive and also destructive. It was that adult part that was able to stand up for myself when I did.

Persistent control tactics can strip our power away to the point where we can be reduced to feeling like a fearful child. Obviously from this position it is extremely difficult to deal with our situation effectively. If this has become an established pattern for you it is important to seek other people's support. Chapter 7 'Becoming More Powerful' contains many strategies to help you to reconnect with your sense of personal power.

Becoming Lost in Searching for Why

> *I didn't see it for what it was. I doubted myself. I wondered what I was doing to bring this about. Where was it going to lead and when was it going to stop? I just wanted to know how to make it stop. I wondered why it had come to this. I kept thinking, 'Why is this happening? What am I doing to deserve this? What am I doing wrong?' I blamed myself. I thought it had to be me. Nothing else made sense.*

Power games often consist of a confusing barrage of activities and accusations that defy logic and leave us shaken and bewildered. If someone is hurting us it is only natural we want to understand why. Most women spend a lot of time trying to fathom this question, but our endless search for the reason often in itself becomes exhausting and disempowering. We may entertain all kinds of possible answers to the 'why' question: high stress, family history, alcohol or drug use, mental illness, jealousy . . . But somehow these answers do not quite ring true. In fact although these things may be contributing factors they are not in themselves the reason for the hurtful behaviour. The truth is that people usually play power games because it meets a need in them. (See Chapter 11 'What Drives Us?' for further discussion of this.)

Sadly, many women eventually begin to believe what they are being told: that the reason the person is hurting them is because they are not measuring up. It is important to realise that regardless of what we are doing or not doing we do not deserve to be treated disrespectfully. At some level the person using power games is making a choice to do so. Although it can be enormously painful to acknowledge this when we do, we are then in a better position to find ways to protect and strengthen ourselves.

Sliding into Depression

I began to feel really hopeless. Like, 'What's the use of trying any more?' I just couldn't get it right and I didn't care any more. I felt so tired and miserable and alone. I thought no-one cared. It was awful.

Depression is a common result of being bullied. The symptoms include very low energy and a sense of hopelessness, poor concentration, low motivation, loss of sex drive, changes in sleeping and/or eating patterns, low flat mood for much of the time and/or possible suicidal thoughts. If you are experiencing some of these symptoms and have had them for two weeks or more you could be suffering from depression. Visit your GP for an assessment and find someone to support you in working through the underlying issues and making changes.

Increasing Anxiety

I became more and more jittery and strung out. I had this awful knot in my gut. I worried about things all the time. I just couldn't get the problems out of my head. I'd be awake at night going over and over things, trying to make sense out of them. When I did finally get to sleep, as soon as I woke up it would all be there again.

Under prolonged stress we often become increasingly on edge and fearful. For some women this anxiety permeates every area of their life. For others the anxiety is very much triggered by the person using power games.

I used to feel absolutely terrified of my boss. Just the power she had to put me down and humiliate me. I became so anxious that I started to make silly mistakes and do clumsy things. When she asked me questions I'd just go completely blank even though I knew the answer. If there were other people around it was even worse. It was so embarrassing.

Deteriorating Health

I got to the stage where I couldn't swallow, I'd lost a lot of weight, I'd had three operations. Every time I threw myself into something fearful like leading the church singing I'd get this lump in my throat. It got harder and harder to push myself into nervous things where I had to take control of myself. I felt so worn out, like my life had been taken away and I was old before my time. My self-esteem and dignity had been stripped.

Ongoing strain on our emotions inevitably affects our physical well-being. Stress can take a huge toll on our bodies, causing physical symptoms such as nausea, headaches, dizziness, sleep disturbances and breathing problems.

Hiding and Displacing Our Anger

I used to feel really resentful a lot of the time. I was just stewing but I did my best to hide it. After all, what was the use of getting into it? It would just be further proof that I was not a nice person.

If we are being hurt, feeling angry is an appropriate, healthy response. However, many of us fear that if we express our anger outwardly we will make our situation worse. Instead we direct our anger at ourselves.

> *I hate myself for being so pathetic and weak. I just don't seem to be able to stand up for myself at all. I'm just too scared, and that in itself is pitiful. It's just too hard to fight any more. I feel worn out with it. No wonder this is happening if I haven't got the guts to stand up for myself.*

For further discussion see 'Women and Anger', p. 99, and 'Use the Energy of Anger', p. 121.

Turning to Power Games Ourselves

> *I got so tormented, and so wound up and uptight that everyone else suffered. All the crap and hassles flowed into my own family. I became this destructive, aggressive person myself. I was getting so angry and frustrated that I'd take it out on my partner. He was copping it all the time. I was hard and cutting. Later on I'd think, 'I didn't want to say that,' but once it's said it's too late. I can think back to some of the hateful, nasty, hurtful things I've said to Paul because of the barrage I was getting from work. I was trying so hard to be nice at work that by the time I got home I was ready to fight with somebody.*

Under the pressure of bullying, however subtle, we may begin to take our anger out on others, often our nearest and dearest. As we act in ways that are against our values we are likely to feel worse.

Children can be a ready target when we are feeling frustrated. If we are taking our hurts out on our children we need to find ways to stop. Children are dependent on us and therefore are vulnerable to us and our moods. They do not deserve to bear the brunt of our anger and pain. See Chapter 12 'Choosing to Change' and 'Stopping Hurtful Behaviour towards Children', p. 255 for ideas for changing destructive behaviour.

Life-long Pain

> *Part of me feels like a little girl that is lost. I actually tell myself now 'I'm an orphan.' That's the only way I feel I can deal with the hurt child inside me. The part of me that is a woman says, 'I want to get on with my life', but I can't ignore the pain. It's still holding me back. I just wish I could squeeze the pain out and it would be gone for good. I don't know if I'll ever get rid of the incredible damage of what's been done to me.*

Healing from the effects of power games can be a long process, especially if destructive power has been directed at us as a child and the impact has been profound. If there is no resolution we may continue to carry that pain for life.

> *I've learned how to work around society's racism. It's really very hard. The distrust remains. No matter how much therapy and how many times I talk about it it's still there. It's very painful to talk about. I'm hurt and it's really hard to forget it and pretend that it's all better. It will never be all better. It's not something that can be forgotten.*

Exercise: Identify the Impact

If we are suffering ongoing power games within the family, workplace or community it is important to take stock of what it is doing to us. One woman clearly described the process of honest soul-searching she went through in order to begin to be able to make some changes in her situation.

> *Recently I've begun to ask myself how much longer I am prepared to go on living under a constant anxiety that affects everything I do. I'm coming to terms with the fact that I can't keep going like*

this. My son is an adult and I now have some understanding that his behaviour affects my whole life. His bullying is not just a discreet little behaviour that turns on and off. It's infiltrated my whole life and being, and my relationships with other people. I always feel anxious and exhausted and that impacts on how I deal with other things in my life. I'm 44. How much longer do I want to keep on dealing with this? I don't want to waste the rest of my life.

To clarify your own situation check (✔) each of the statements you relate to and put a question mark (?) beside those you partially relate to.

Due to the stress of power games:

_____ My confidence and self-esteem are decreasing.

_____ I am trying harder and harder to please to avoid conflict.

_____ I often feel anxious, afraid and/or trapped.

_____ I often feel helpless, hopeless and/or depressed.

_____ I have given up many of the things I used to enjoy.

_____ I feel too ashamed to tell other people what is happening.

_____ I increasingly feel like a child rather than a competent adult.

_____ I spend a lot of time trying to understand why this is happening.

_____ I am becoming increasingly hard on myself.

_____ I often feel confused and sometimes I'm afraid I'm going crazy.

_____ My relationships with other people are suffering.

_____ I'm becoming increasingly burnt out.

_____ I am suffering physical symptoms of stress.

_____ I am using alcohol, drugs and/or too much food to help me cope.

_____ The standard of my work is slipping because of the pressure I'm under.

_____ I'm too afraid to stand up to the person who is hurting me.

_____ I am beginning to take my stress out on other people.

Having completed this checklist you may want to explore the following questions in your journal:

▶ What is it like to identify honestly the impact that power games are having on you?

▶ How are you feeling?

▶ What have you realised after reading this chapter?

Gaining an awareness of the effect of the power games in your life can be unsettling. Sharing your insights with your support person can help. Using some of the self-care suggestions on p. 210 and p. 230 may also help.

The most important information to take from this chapter is that it is quite normal for our self-esteem to slip and our behaviour to change if we are being frequently undermined. Therefore we need to practise giving up self-blame and forgive ourselves for any ways we have compromised our integrity. While it can be sad to realise the ways we have changed, this realisation can act as a vital incentive for us to begin to reclaim our power.

CHAPTER 6

What Contributes to Our Powerlessness?

I n the previous chapter women shared their confusion and pain at being the target of others' hurtful power. People who have not experienced the devastation of power games tend to believe that dealing with bullying – whether it is in the home, the workplace or the community – is a straightforward and simple matter of standing our ground, confronting, complaining to the authorities or leaving. Those of us who have experienced ongoing power plays first hand know just how challenging it is to handle this bewildering, complex and soul-destroying experience effectively.

This chapter addresses the question of why many women find it so difficult to deal with the bullying in their lives in powerful ways. It focuses on three factors that often contribute to our sense of powerlessness: our female conditioning, the disempowering coping strategies we often adopt, and the impact of our personal history. At the end of each section there is a list of questions to help you to assess the influence that this particular factor is having on you.

OUR FEMALE CONDITIONING

As women we carry society's expectations that we will be 'good', 'kind' and 'nice' – the caretakers, nurturers, givers, peacemakers – 'ever-flowing breasts' for those around us: our children, partners, parents, friends, neighbours, colleagues and community. Being 'good' means being passive and accepting other people's demands without protest. Small wonder many of us feel under pressure and find it difficult to defy our conditioning, stand up for ourselves and say no to people who would exploit us.

Women are experts at attending to others: noticing the small nuances that give a clue to their moods, monitoring their feeling states and anticipating their needs and desires. Our possession of this 'sensitivity' is one of the characteristics of a 'good' woman. Our sensitivity carries a cost, however. Busy tuning in to those around us, we often overlook our own needs.

When we do, often belatedly, recognise our needs, the task of attending to them is usually scheduled for after we have met other people's requirements. This inevitably means many of our needs are never met. In fact we are taught that the needs of others, especially men and children, are more important than ours. To put ourselves first and ask for what we want is often seen as 'selfish' – by ourselves as well as other people.

As we have seen, it is common for the domineering person to attack our performance and accuse us of not being 'good enough'. This matches perfectly with women's common experience of not being 'good enough' to meet the impossible standards set for them by society. Rather than identifying the overpowering person's demands as excessive and their accusations as insulting, we can easily fall into the trap of trying harder to prove we are okay. But our efforts to please are doomed to failure. The agenda of the person doing the bullying is usually to maintain a 'one up' position, so whatever we do we are given the message that we are still not doing it right. As we unsuccessfully try to measure up we are likely to become increasing burnt out and disillusioned.

The majority of women who become worn down and overwhelmed by power struggles do not identify the role that female conditioning plays in this. It is true that men who are subjected to repeated bullying will also usually lose confidence and personal power. But women tend to lose ground more quickly and profoundly. Our conditioning to be obliging, compassionate and giving means we are predisposed to accommodate rather than confront. Most men live by very different rules to women. Conditioning teaches them to be goal oriented, single-minded and in control: to achieve, compete and win at all costs and to regard themselves as leaders and decision-makers. Thus they are inclined to deal with power games in a more forthright and aggressive manner.

Exercise: How Do We Give Our Power Away?

Not only does our female conditioning make it challenging to stand up against others' control, it can also cause us to give away what power we do have. Some of the ways we often unthinkingly deplete our power are listed below. Check (✔) each one you recognise as true for you and place a question mark (?) beside those that are sometimes true.

I deplete my power by:

_____ not giving myself enough rest, relaxation, fun, solitude or nurturing;

_____ putting myself down, blaming and criticising myself harshly;

_____ being unwilling or unable to accept praise and compliments;

_____ setting myself up for failure by striving to be and do things perfectly;

_____ refusing to accept my limitations, mistakes and human frailties;

_____ trying to please others for fear they won't like or approve of me;

_____ avoiding speaking my truth because I'm afraid of upsetting other people;

_____ focusing on helping/rescuing others instead of looking after my own needs;

_____ telling myself I'm not as good as other people;

_____ staying invisible: not expressing opinions, ideas, feelings or thoughts;

_____ agreeing, apologising and pretending I'm okay when I'm not;

_____ not acknowledging when I'm upset or angry about something;

_____ letting myself be manipulated, taken advantage of and mistreated;

_____ waiting for other people to guess my needs instead of asking for help;

_____ complaining and grumbling without taking appropriate action.

Questions to Consider:

◗ How do you deplete your power?

◗ Is this an established pattern of behaviour?

◗ When you give your power away what is the effect on you?

◗ Are there changes you would like to make?

◗ What would this involve?

Women and Relationships

Building and maintaining good relationships is central to our identity as women. If our relationships are in a state of conflict (for whatever reason) we are inclined to take too much responsibility for this and work harder to 'make things right'. Instead of being clear when the other person's behaviour is out of line we may automatically make allowances for them and slip into the caretaking role.

> *My boss was short-tempered, nasty and always on my back, yet I made all kinds of excuses for him. I told myself he was having a rough time at the moment, his wife was sick, we had a lot of work on and I knew he was tired. I had my own problems, that's for sure, but somehow his seemed more important and I felt sorry for him, like I should help him out and let him off the hook.*

In our intimate relationships we may go one step further and believe that our love has the power to work the miracle of healing and to transform a destructive relationship into a respectful one. We may also believe that if we love 'enough' we will be loved in return. Our determination to reach out, to heal or love someone 'better' can keep us caught in a life-draining spiral of self-sacrifice and helplessness.

> *Gail was horrible to me a lot but I knew she was in pain and she'd never got over what her father had done to her. I made excuses because I really loved her and I just wanted it to work out. I wanted to believe in the nice part of her, so that was what I tried to focus on. I really thought if I kept loving her she'd love me back and be kind to me. I just wanted her to see that I was there for her and I honestly thought that would heal her. I can now see that was totally unrealistic.*

While we can offer each other support and comfort the reality is each of us must do our own individual healing work if we are to free ourselves from a past that is haunting us.

There are many societal, spiritual and religious messages that inform women about their role in relationships and encourage us to put up with destructive behaviour while continuing to strive for improvement. We are told:

▶ Turn the other cheek.
▶ Forgive and forget.
▶ We get back what we give out.
▶ Love your enemies.
▶ You can change a relationship by changing your thoughts.
▶ You have attracted this destructive situation into your life to learn lessons from.
▶ Other people's bad behaviour is a mirror of our own unacknowledged feelings.
▶ You made your bed, you lie in it.
▶ Love can conquer all.
▶ The path of true love never runs smooth.
▶ Stand by your man.

Beliefs like these can have a powerful underlying effect on the way we feel compelled to act, as the following woman's story highlights.

My spiritual beliefs were that if I was good, I would receive good, and if I was honest, honesty would come back to me. I believed it with such conviction: that was my faith and I clung to it. I loved my partner so much I should have had the most amazing love back. I thought that if I believed hard enough it would happen. When it all came tumbling down I thought that all of my beliefs were stuffed because none of what I believed had happened. I'd tried so hard to do everything that I thought I should – being positive, being committed, being honest – but it hadn't worked. That was my foundation for everything, for every belief system I had. And all of a sudden I had to acknowledge that it didn't work and I had nothing, absolutely nothing to have faith in. It never occurred to me I could have faith in myself. I realise now that those beliefs were very restricting in that they put a lot of pressure on me because I was always trying to be good, otherwise in my mind I didn't deserve to get any of the things I wanted. I had handed out all my power. I believed that it was 'out there'. I didn't believe in myself enough. That's so damaging.

Religious doctrine is often also interpreted in ways that are disabling to women.

For years one of the reasons I accepted what my husband said and did was because I had this incorrect image of a Christian wife as submissive. Submissive to me meant if my husband wanted some-thing then I had to agree. Then I realised when I was talking to a friend that my ideas were wrong. I had misinterpreted them. That was one of the reasons I began to see things for what they really were and realise that this was not right.

It is not uncommon for women guided by spiritual principles to continue to reach out in loving kindness in the hope that the aggressor will respond to them in the same manner. But often the bullying behaviour escalates in response.

For a long time I felt confident that I could win over the people at work because I had read all these spiritual books about how to do things lovingly, so I just kept reaching out and being nice. But it just didn't work. I was just too nice. I was so compliant they couldn't believe their luck.

Questions to Consider

▶ Does the person who is using power games appear to hold negative beliefs and attitudes about women?

▶ Do you hold certain beliefs that are contributing to your disempowerment? What are these?

- Are you inclined to take too much responsibility and to overcompensate for the other person's lack of input by working too hard to make things right?
- Do you believe that your needs are important?
- Have you become so focused on the person who is doing the harm that you have lost sight of your own needs?

Women and Mothering

Women are under extraordinary pressure from society to be 'good' mothers: maternal, ever-patient, kind and self-sacrificing home-makers and childcarers. Often we strive unconsciously to meet this impossible ideal, then when we fall short we automatically feel like a failure and give ourselves a hard time.

Our success in the mothering role is usually measured by our ability to produce 'good' children. If our child's behaviour is far from 'good' and he or she is being destructive towards us we are likely to be left feeling inadequate and impotent in our mothering role.

> *My son's bullying has undermined my self-esteem as a mother. It's been hard letting go of the thought that I'm the one who can make things right for my son, I'm the one who can help him reach his potential. I long to help him. That feeling is so powerful. It feels really frustrating not to be able to do it. The whole concept of being a mother, being supportive, giving another chance, providing a home, has kept me hanging in there. There is always that in the background. It's very hard to let go of the ideal that families should be together. How am I supposed to be? What am I doing to make this family a family? I feel conflicted as a woman. His behaviour has been a shock, because I just hate violence, especially against women. To me it is just an atrocity.*

When people see a child behaving destructively some automatically assume that the reason is 'bad parenting'. As women are primarily responsible for children this translates to 'bad mothering' and sets us up for guilt and self-blame. Our sense of shame and fear of other people's judgement can be a real barrier to reaching out for help when we need it.

It is easy to overlook the fact that children are socialised not only by mothers but by fathers, grandparents, aunts, uncles, the school system, neighbours, friends and the community. If a child is behaving badly it can be for a number of reasons that are completely outside our responsibility and control. (See 'Defusing Destructive Power Struggles', p. 252, and 'Dealing with Children's Hurtful Behaviour', p. 259 for suggestions on how to deal with this.)

Women and Blame

Inside the family where power games are played by a father, children often direct their anger and blame at their mother. She is a less threatening target.

> Mum was the protector and the peacemaker. Anything at all costs.
> I lost respect for Mum and got angry at her quite a lot because I
> always thought, 'Why are you putting up with this? Why don't
> you leave him?' Around my father I was totally passive because I
> was scared of him. I stood up to him a couple of times, but that
> was all. There was just this constant striving for his approval.

It is not uncommon for children to hold their mothers responsible for their father's bullying, blaming her for being passive. This is a reflection of society's tendency to blame women for power games that other people choose to play. This blame is reflected in assumptions many people make about relationships in which women are being abused, such as:

▶ 'She must have done something to deserve it.'
▶ 'She must have provoked him.'

- ◗ 'She hasn't left so it can't be that bad.'
- ◗ 'It's her own fault because she puts up with it.'
- ◗ 'She doesn't stand up for herself so she must like it.'
- ◗ 'She is attracting this abuse into her life.'

This blaming way of thinking puts the focus on the woman and what she is doing or not doing, instead of on the other person's inappropriate behaviour. This implies that she is responsible for the destructive behaviour. *In fact the person using the power tactics makes the choice to do this and needs to be held accountable.* Nevertheless, many women constantly encounter these attitudes, sometimes in very overt ways.

> *My family didn't particularly like my husband. He was physically and verbally violent and they knew that but they blamed me. They believed that if he was hitting me there must be a reason. I must have asked to be beaten up. I must have provoked him, and if I stayed there I must have liked it. Then when I did separate they were quite blaming and judgemental. According to my family I had made my bed so I had to lie in it and I wasn't to expect any help from them. I'd blown it by choosing badly.*

By claiming that 'it's her own fault' and that they themselves would never put up with it, people avoid facing the fact that this could happen to them. It is uncomfortable to acknowledge that any of us could become a victim of violence, sickness, poverty or other adversities. It is safer to hold the view that the person brought it on themselves than to admit that they may be an innocent party.

Women and Anger
We have an absolute right to feel angry when someone is deliberately hurting us – in fact it is natural to feel angry if our well-being is

threatened. However, as women we are constantly given the message that anger is not acceptable. Women who display anger are often named as 'bitches', 'nags', 'stroppy' or 'aggressive'. This puts us in a double bind: if we allow ourselves to get angry and express this we are accused of being unfeminine and wrong. Alternatively, if we deny our anger and keep it bottled up inside we are depriving ourselves of the very energy that could enable us to take action on our own behalf. The following story clearly illustrates the link between denial of anger and powerlessness.

> *The nurses' socialisation as women played a significant role in the way they responded to being bullied. They were always supportive. They would get distressed and upset and sad but very few of them would get angry. I'd try to get them to recognise anger in themselves, but anger was not an emotion that they identified. As women we are not allowed to show anger. The other big thing was the fear of labels. If you were assertive or confident you were labelled as being aggressive. That was used against any nurse who stood outside the passive, supportive, compliant role.*

Questions to Consider

▶ How comfortable are you with your anger? If you felt angry towards someone would you usually:

   hide your anger behind silence or a smile?

   behave hurtfully towards the person concerned?

   let off steam to someone else but say nothing to the person concerned?

   convert your anger into tears?

   not address the problem directly but become offhand or sarcastic instead?

   express your anger assertively, yet respectfully?

▶ When you are angry do you tend to turn it on yourself rather than express it to the person concerned?

▶ Do you numb out your anger by overeating or using alcohol or drugs?

▶ Do you sometimes take your anger out on someone non-threatening rather than expressing it directly to the person concerned?

▶ What fears do you have about expressing your anger directly? Are you afraid:

others will see you as aggressive?

the other person will retaliate?

you will lose control and do or say things you will regret?

you will rock the boat?

you will hurt someone?

you will become bitter?

you will feel guilty and wrong for feeling angry?

(For further discussion on expressing anger see 'Strategies for Harnessing Anger', p. 121, and 'Become More Assertive', p. 129.)

Women and Deference

As women we have been socialised to minimise our own accomplishments and those of other women and to defer to men's knowledge and authority. When men with power are around us we may fade into the background, forgetting the fact that we have valid knowledge that may be equal or superior to that of the men we are deferring to. Needless to say, if we see ourselves as inferior to men who decide to bully us we will have little in the way of protection or power against them.

> When the doctors weren't there the nurses assumed a much higher profile in their role. They made major decisions, they were highly skilled in what they did and interactive with families and other staff, extremely professional and very competent. It was just this dynamic with the doctors. There would be a shift. It was so distressing.

Sadly, women can sometimes be other women's harshest critics and most aggressive rivals. We may feel distrustful toward other women. To help us feel more powerful we may join with society's criticisms of women and even openly state that we don't like women. We may try to distance ourselves from other women and our own identity as a woman by dismissing them as weak.

> *Until recently I couldn't stand women. I used to think they were silly bitches, really petty and dull and boring. I do have women friends now but even so I much prefer men because I like men's company much better than women's. They're so much more interesting. I just feel good being around them. I bypass women as much as possible and deal with men instead if I can. It's much more fun.*

Questions to Consider

▶ Are there times when you defer to men's knowledge and decisions, even when you know more and want something different?

▶ Are you proud to be a woman or do you align yourself more closely with men?

▶ If the latter, why do you think this is?

▶ How would you describe a successful woman? Are the terms you use affirming or derogatory?

▶ How would you describe a successful man? Are the terms you use affirming or derogatory?

▶ Is there any difference between the two descriptions? If so, why is this?

▶ Are you satisfied with your relationships with other women?

▶ If not, how would you like these relationships to change?

▶ What can you do to assist this to happen?

THE COPING STRATEGIES WE USE

As we have seen coping with power games, whether in the home, workplace or community, changes us. The ongoing impact can erode our confidence and self-esteem and wear us down to the point of mental confusion and emotional and physical exhaustion. We begin to feel insecure and discouraged, we lose our self-respect and become increasingly defeated.

To protect ourselves from the misery and stress of our situation we often slip into ways of coping that seem to help. We may play down the seriousness of our situation or pretend we don't have a problem at all. We may use selective memory to focus on the good times and forget the bad. We may try harder and harder in the hope that we can somehow manage to make things right. In the short term these mental tricks and coping strategies seem to offer some small comfort. They may help us get through another day or hide our distress, but in the longer term they compound the problem by preventing us from facing the situation honestly and taking appropriate action.

There are a number of coping strategies that women typically adopt to help them survive. The following seven women share their memories of what they did to make their lives more bearable.

Denying What Is Happening

> *I was locked into such denial for so long. Partly this was because I couldn't see the wood for the trees, but also I just didn't want to face the facts and see what was happening. The shame and humiliation of acknowledging the truth, even to myself, was more than I could bear.*

Failing to See the Behaviour for What It Is

> *At first I didn't give Vicky's abuse a name and that made it so much*

harder to deal with. I still tend to water it down by saying, 'She's not that bad,' but really her behaviour is very manipulative and destructive.

Taking the Blame on Ourselves

I was bewildered more than anything. I just didn't understand what was going on. I thought I'd lost the plot somewhere. It didn't make sense. I just felt hurt and I blamed myself. What's wrong with me? What have I done? I felt embarrassed about the whole thing. I kept trying to make the situation right. It was a job I knew and loved. I didn't want to give it up. It was a challenge: I thought I'd work at it. Surely if I kept doing the right things it would work out? Perhaps if I'd become angry they would have respected me more. But I felt inadequate and I took it on myself instead.

Holding On to Hope Too Long

If Geoff gives me any hope I'll latch on to it. Any little flicker of humour or anything, I reach out and grasp onto it. It lulls me into a false security. If the day after a blow-up Geoff is co-operative the whole thing is almost blocked out of my mind and I think, 'No, this is the way it really is. He's really not that bad.' Until it happens again. I recognise now that that's a process I go through.

Making Excuses for the Behaviour

My son's behaviour dominates the whole house. We are coping with it all day, yet I've thought of every excuse rather than deal with it. I'd make excuses to his brother like, 'You know, Kerry hasn't got as many social skills or friends as you.' I've wondered if something happened in the womb when I was given antibiotics. I've always given him another chance and another chance but he just isn't owning his behaviour and I've come to realise that if I allow it to go on without doing something then I'm saying it's okay. In some ways I've already been condoning his behaviour. I accepted it because I was his mother and I thought I owed him, even though I was saying to him, 'I don't like you doing this because I'm afraid that you'll go and do it to other women.' But I wasn't really acting on my concerns so nothing actually changed.

Trying Too Hard

I was so absorbed in my work. It just took so much of my energy and I was so overloaded that I didn't have anything left for anybody or anything, but my boss still kept piling the work on. I took work home with me most nights and worried about things all the time. In amongst all of the stress I totally lost touch with myself and my feelings. My body was trying to tell me I was in overdrive with headaches and backaches but I wouldn't take any notice. I put all my time and energy into trying to stay on top and second-guess him. My work became my whole life. It was like nothing else mattered but proving to this domineering man that I was okay and could do the work. It was crazy.

Becoming Silenced

I eventually got to the stage where I never went out. I withdrew into myself and became more silent. I stopped reading books and newspapers because if I read then I'd want to talk about them. I lived in my own world. It got to the stage where I actually found it difficult to speak because I'd withdrawn so much I couldn't

> *actually talk to people. When they asked me questions I felt I couldn't respond, I didn't know how to.*

It is easy to see how denial, confusion, self-blame, hoping against the facts, excusing bad behaviour, striving to please and losing our voice feed the powerlessness we often experience when we are caught in another's power games.

There may be many other unhelpful strategies we adopt in an effort to protect ourselves, including:

❱ becoming secretive and withdrawn from others to hide our shame;

❱ drinking, taking drugs or overeating to numb the pain;

❱ giving up the things we used to enjoy in order to keep the peace or conserve what is left of our energy.

Exercise: Clarify Your Coping Strategies

It is important that we clarify what coping strategies we have been using. That way we can assess whether these strategies are truly serving us and, if not, decide whether we want to abandon them in favour of more empowering ways of coping. Which of the following statements about the dynamics of coping with power games do you identify with? Check (✔) each statement that is true for you, or if it is partially true mark it with a question mark (?).

___✔___ I have tended to deny the seriousness of what is happening because it is too difficult to face.

___✔___ I have not clearly recognised or acknowledged that what I am experiencing is a form of abuse.

___✔___ I have taken on the blame for the problems.

___✔___ I have persisted in holding on to hope even when there was little (or no) basis for it.

_____ I have often excused destructive behaviour.

___✔___ I have resorted to trying too hard to 'get it right'.

____ I have shut down and resorted to silence as a way of
        protecting myself.

List any other ways you have changed in an attempt to cope.

Questions to Consider

▶ What is the cost to you of using these strategies?

▶ Are they undermining your ability to act on your own behalf?

▶ What fears (if any) do you have about giving up these coping
   strategies?

▶ What might be the gains of doing this?

▶ Do you need help to change any self-defeating behaviours?

THE IMPACT OF OUR PERSONAL HISTORY

Our initial lessons about power came from our family of origin. What
we saw demonstrated there is likely to have a big impact on our
current sense of power or lack or it. Our early experiences taught us
about who had power, how it was maintained and how it could be used
or abused.

We may have grown up in a family where freedom of speech,
diverse ideas and personal privacy were respected and family members
were encouraged to be individuals and allowed to be different. In this
type of family we learn to think for ourselves and use our feelings,
ideas, thoughts and preferences as a guide to the choices we make. We
develop the confidence to speak out and feel entitled to be treated with
respect.

Unfortunately many of us grew up in less than ideal circumstances
where an atmosphere of power struggles, hostility and helplessness
was the norm. In this kind of family the rights and needs of individuals
are overlooked or ignored. For many of us these lessons set the scene
for ongoing confusion, doubts and fears about power in our lives.
Three women share their experiences:

> My father was very controlling and his anger was vented at me.
> He never hit me but I lived in absolute fear of him. The only
> expression of anything I was allowed to portray was total
> compliance, total obedience. If he said the moon was blue, it was
> blue: his word was law, regardless.

> Right from when I was very young my mother read all my mail
> and listened to all my phone calls. She'd always get jealous of my
> friends and get really abusive. Everyone I ever introduced her to
> was never good enough, so I couldn't have a friend. I felt like I was
> a caged animal and I couldn't get away.

> I just hated my brother. We fought all the time, but I was two years
> younger so I'd come off worst. He was always hounding me and
> getting me into trouble and bashing me and telling me I was not
> part of the family, locking me outside at night when Mum and Dad
> weren't there.

For some of us the parenting we received was invasive and
oppressive. Our privacy was violated, our personal boundaries were
not respected and our freedom was rigidly controlled.

> My father played with me just like a cat plays with a mouse. I'd
> sit in my room to swot and he'd just burst the door open to check
> on me all the time. If I went to the toilet he'd immediately try the
> handle of the door, not to come in for any perverted reasons, but
> to let me know he was there. Even if he'd just been to the toilet he'd
> pretend he wanted to go again. If I used the toaster he'd scream,
> 'Who's used the toaster?' even though he knew it was me. I'd sit
> in the lounge at night watching for his car headlights. When I saw
> them, that was it. I went to my room to stay out of his way.

Some of us emerged from childhood feeling powerless for a different reason: we were smothered by an emotionally over-involved parent. We were indulged, over-protected and rescued: our concerns were taken care of, our decisions made, our problems solved and our battles fought. When we are over-parented in these ways we are constantly given the message that we are incompetent, helpless, in need of protection and unable to think for ourselves. We are taught we can't make it on our own. This makes it difficult to develop a sense of competence, autonomy or independence – all important aspects of personal power.

The impact of parenting that is neglectful, wounding, oppressive or smothering can be far-reaching, as the following three women's stories show.

> When I'm around my mother I immediately begin to think how stupid and ugly I am. It's just habitual. She doesn't need to say or do anything: she's said and done it all before. That's what frightens me. I just do it to myself now. I start to bring myself down and absolutely hate myself. The greatest hurt is that no-one believes and no-one understands what my mother has done to me. Even I don't fully understand. It is frightening to acknowledge that my mother is my enemy, and the loneliest part of it is that no-one thinks that a mother can betray you. Sometimes I want to believe it is all a big lie and that she hasn't been so cruel to me, but she has.

> My destructive relationship with my father has created a tendency to have relationships that are unhealthy, with a lack of trust, a lot of self-denial and self-hatred. I don't have a very strong sense of self. I have a problem with boundaries, a problem with being able to speak honestly. I have had a problem with not being in touch with myself and my feelings. For years I was not really grounded and I suffered from depression. Everything was just grey.

I feel like the whole of my life I've had this all-consuming fear that has affected everything. It's tied me up in knots. I've survived by controlling situations, manipulating people, making sure that I was safe. I think everything is my fault. I watch other people all the time, especially their eyes. Do they like me? Don't they like me? It has brought a real insecurity into my life and all I can do at times is to try to push that to one side. Everything I do is slightly nervous and I think as the years have gone on I've become much more sensitive to atmospheres and people. If someone yells at me in a job I'm a blithering idiot. Everything affects my gut.

Our past may continue to haunt us and be replayed in many guises. Our old powerless feelings can be recreated almost automatically when we find ourselves in a challenging situation.

My bullying boss reminded me so much of my father. It was awful when he stood over me for making a mistake or blamed me for misplacing papers I hadn't even seen. I'd feel so small – just like I was a kid again, crying to my father and trying to explain that I hadn't done it.

As we have seen, the misuse of power by parents may not end when we grow into adults. Power games may continue to be used to manipulate us into feeling guilty and inadequate.

My mother uses emotional blackmail all the time. 'I'm stuck here and I can't get out and you don't care. I'm sick and you don't even come to see me. Your father would turn in his grave if he knew how you treated me.' It's all rubbish but it makes me feel absolutely worthless. I just can't do it right.

Most parents do the best they can for their children. It can be enormously challenging to face the reality that for whatever reason our parent has not been able to give us the care and love we need.

Acknowledging this is not about blaming. It is about being honest with ourselves over the issues we are struggling with. While we continue to deny the impact of our past we are at risk of repeating past patterns. To heal these hurts we need to take time to work through the sadness and anger we feel when we fully realise what we have never had. (See 'Healing Past Hurts', p. 233, for a further discussion of this.)

Questions to Consider

▶ In your family of origin who had the most power?

▶ Was there a 'pecking order'? Where did you fit in? How was that for you?

▶ As a child did you witness or experience power expressed in respectful ways? How did this influence you?

▶ Did you witness or experience power expresses in destructive ways? What impact did this have on you?

▶ In what ways was your power undermined as a child?

▶ Were you encouraged to feel that your needs were important and your concerns mattered, or were your needs overlooked or diminished?

▶ Were your efforts, feelings, budding ideas and attempts at independence treated with sensitivity and respect or ignored, stifled or ridiculed?

▶ Were you encouraged to develop a sense of confidence, competence and responsibility or were you over-protected by an anxious or over-involved parent?

▶ What effect have your early experiences had on you and your expression of power?

▶ Are there still issues of power in your relationships with members of your family of origin today?

▶ Are parts of your personal history being replayed in your current situation in any way?

▶ Do you need to work through painful memories of your childhood?

In this chapter we have considered how our female conditioning, self-defeating coping strategies and personal history may be contributing to our sense of powerlessness. Although obviously anybody would begin to lose confidence if they were subjected to ongoing power games, these factors can add to our burden in effectively dealing with our situation. The more aware we are of these influences the more we can find ways to overcome our fears and take the necessary steps to protect ourselves.

Reflecting on how these particular issues relate to you may have stirred up feelings of sadness, anger or anxiety. If so, it is important to take good care of yourself. Talk through these feelings with your support person and/or write about them in your journal. Also practise some of the self-care suggestions on p. 231. In the next chapter we will explore ways of regaining our power in the face of other people's power games.

CHAPTER 7

Becoming More Powerful

Finding and claiming our power can be a big challenge if we are feeling crushed by power games. We may have felt strong and reasonably confident before experiencing the oppression of power games, or we may have had a lifetime of feeling powerless and at the bottom of the heap in our personal lives as well as in the outside world. Either way, becoming a more powerful woman is an ongoing journey. This journey involves discovering our inner strength and learning to express it in ways that honour our right to be treated with respect, and to live a life that is independent, safe and meaningful for us. Over time there are many steps we can take and changes we can make on this journey.

Becoming more powerful begins with a shift in our thinking: a clear decision to protect and champion ourselves, to put ourselves and our well-being first and do what is right for us. The dictates of self-sacrifice are often embedded deep in women's psyches and we may enact our role unconsciously. We have seen that as women we often face the ongoing challenge of defying the conditioning that says we should put others first, deciding instead to act on our own behalf. This is a big move. Reclaiming our power requires breaking through society's constraints and honouring ourselves as the unique women we are.

In fact we are usually far more powerful than we realise. Think about it. As women we can often muster enormous power and courage to act on behalf of our children or friends, yet become doubting and timid when it comes to ourselves. To make a change we need to begin to own, embrace and use the power we *do have* to support ourselves in our personal lives, in the workplace and in the wider community.

It may sound daunting to imagine the possibility of becoming more powerful in every aspect of our lives, but we don't need to do it all at once. Claiming our power is a process of small steps – small acts by which we set our boundaries, refuse to be treated disrespectfully and take action to protect ourselves and enhance our lives.

This chapter looks at a number of ideas and strategies to help you increase your personal power. Women also share their experiences of discovering their inner strength and taking a stand against power games within close relationships, the workplace and community. Gradually over time these women have been able to regain control over their lives and make positive changes.

As you work your way through this chapter and try out some of the suggestions, be gentle with yourself. Choose the strategies you feel comfortable with and move at a pace that best suits you. Remember to acknowledge your efforts as well as your successes. When we are feeling overwhelmed, taking even one small step to challenge and change the situation can be a big victory. Each small step does make a difference, as the women on the following pages show.

Put the Responsibility Where It Belongs

Our tendency as women to take too much responsibility for conflicted relationships does not serve us well. Self-blame is destructive and debilitating. It clouds the issue and acts as a deterrent to our taking positive action. When we are on the receiving end of power games it is vital that we are clear that the other person is responsible for his or her actions, not us.

> *I think what is really important is to shift out of it personally. It's not about thinking, 'What did I do to get that?' It is about asking, 'What happened there?' Removing ourselves from the bullying behaviour, because it is not to do with us personally. It's about the dynamic. It's looking back and saying, 'That behaviour towards me is unacceptable.' Even if we can't put a label on it we can say, 'I don't want that person to behave like that towards me and I have a right to not have to experience that in my workplace.'*

It can be a challenge to put the responsibility back to the hurtful person because in doing so we then need to give up the personal struggle to make things 'right'. We will also need to face the fact that they may not be prepared to take responsibility for their behaviours and change. *Choosing to stop using power destructively is a decision that only that person can make and ultimately we have no control over this.* It can be painful to realise that there may be little we can do to improve the situation if the other person chooses to continue their destructive behaviour. Our main responsibility then needs to be our own self-protection and well-being.

Questions to Consider

▶ Am I taking more than my share of responsibility for the problems?

▶ Am I blaming myself for the hurtful behaviour I am experiencing?

▶ Is the person who is hurting me willing to take responsibility for his/her behaviour?

▶ What fears do I have about putting the responsibility where it belongs?

- ❿ Am I willing to let go of the struggle to put things 'right' and let things run their course?
- ❿ What will this mean for me?

Focus on Yourself

People using power games demand our attention, energy and time. Their needs are pressing, ours unimportant. Days can be lost by focusing on the other person, trying to understand their behaviour. The futility of this feeds our sense of helplessness and fear. In this situation women often describe a sense of losing touch with who they are. This contributes to their feelings of powerlessness. To stop this life-draining cycle it is important to bring our focus back to ourselves. Writing can be a useful tool for this.

> *One of the ways that I managed to cope during the time my boss was bullying me was that each day I came home I'd write in a journal. I'd write my pain and sorrow out and that was the only way I could express something and be heard because at least I was being heard by myself.*

When we find ourselves involved in a power struggle we need to decide what is right for us and how we want to react. If we stay connected to ourselves and think about what we want and need we will be more likely to act on our own behalf. This will help to prevent us from being pulled into conflict situations where we are set up to lose our dignity and self-respect. This change in focus will also allow us to gain some distance from the impact of the other person's hurtful behaviour and help us to see it clearly for what it is: a choice that he or she makes about how to behave, for which we are not responsible.

> *I've had to go inside and find my strength. What's come out of it for me is that I've had to discover my true personal power. My neighbours' bullying stuff doesn't affect me as much now. I had a*

huge shift after I got over the fact that they would do this to me. I realised that by reacting the only person I was going to upset was myself. I'm 45 and I realised I don't need to let them treat me like a child. So I made a conscious choice to accept the situation and not get uptight about it. Otherwise I'd probably have had a nervous breakdown three years ago. I tried to be totally non-reactive because I thought that was probably the most frustrating thing I could do. Also I didn't want to stoop to their level. It was important to rise above it and put my energy into looking after myself.

Questions to Consider

Think of a current situation where you are often on the receiving end of power games. Ask yourself the following questions:

▶ How do I usually feel?

▶ What are my needs, wants and desires in this situation?

▶ How would I act if I were acting in my own best interests?

▶ If I am honest what do I want to do?

▶ Do I want to do something differently now?

▶ What might stop me doing that?

▶ If I choose to do something different what support do I need?

Give Up Guilt

Feeling guilty can be very disempowering. There are two kinds of guilt. Firstly there is realistic guilt, which acts as a signal that we have done wrong. If we use this feeling as a signal we may then choose to act on it by rectifying the situation and perhaps making amends. Secondly there is unrealistic guilt, which comes about when we are blamed (by ourselves or others) for things that are not our responsibility.

As we have seen, guilt often features strongly in women's lives, and this can make us an easy target for people who want to manipulate us. We often feel guilty for things that are outside our control and responsibility. We need not feel guilty if we do not succeed in measuring up to other people's unrealistic expectations for us to be perfect. If we have been true to ourselves and have done what we could within our own limits, that is all other people have the right to expect.

In the following quote a woman shares her struggle with unrealistic guilt. Her decision to give the responsibility for her daughter's destructive behaviour back to her daughter has had powerful results. (For further discussion about power struggles with children see 'Defusing Destructive Power Struggles', p. 252.)

> *When I asked my daughter to leave I felt really guilty but it was the beginning of me allowing myself to separate from someone who was intimidating and bullying me. I was frightened of her and also frightened for her because I could see that she was out of control, but I eventually began to realise that I had the right to save myself. That was a turning point for me. I refused to live with her any more. Lesley went out and lived on her own and went through a series of disasters. I used to think, 'Oh God, I should be there for her, I should rescue her.' But in all of that I knew that the bottom line was that I couldn't live with this person. I just felt so destroyed by her that I couldn't function. I realised that it wasn't good for her and it wasn't good for me. After she left she put a lot of effort into manipulating me and trying to make me feel guilty, saying things like, 'You've abandoned me. You've done this, you've done that to me'. Even though deep down I did feel desperately guilty I held my ground. That was very hard but suddenly it has all begun to change. She's begun to take responsibility for her life and treats me with more respect. I'd started to think it would never happen.*

Questions to Consider

As we work at reclaiming our power it is important to distinguish between our realistic and unrealistic guilt feelings so we are not at the mercy of our own and others' blame. As both types of guilt feel similar it is sometimes difficult to tell the difference. When feeling guilty, try stepping back from the situation and asking yourself the following questions:

▶ Have I acted in keeping with my values?
▶ Have I acted with goodwill and integrity?
▶ Have I deliberately hurt someone?
▶ Do I need to do anything to put matters right?
▶ Whose responsibility (and problem) is this?
▶ Is the other person putting demands on me that are unrealistic or excessive?
▶ Am I being too hard on myself?
▶ Have I done the best I can in the situation?
▶ Am I being true to myself?

Build Your Support

Whether we are experiencing power games in the home, workplace or community one of the most vital steps to take to empower ourselves is to reach out to people who will support us. We need other people to listen to our hurt, encourage and validate us and help us decide what action to take.

I began to regain some power as soon as I allowed the mask to drop and started to communicate with other people. It was only when I began to reach out and talk about what was happening that I began to gain some clarity and strength. I confided in people I could trust and that started the doors opening. Through talking I could see my confused feelings outside myself and hear other people's input. It was just too confusing trying to deal with everything myself. I can now see that suffering in silence was so disempowering because I was terribly confused. How could I sort myself out when I was hiding from the truth and I didn't even know that I was hiding?

Speaking out involves risk. We may be afraid that others are going to look down on us and judge us. Obviously certain people are going to be more supportive than others. Some may disbelieve, blame, judge, patronise or feel out of their depth; others will listen with an open heart and offer invaluable validation and support. It is important to be discriminating when choosing someone to confide in. Women who have been through similar difficulties themselves are likely to be understanding and helpful. Talking to a counsellor or a professional from a helping agency can also be valuable.

Joining with other women in groups also offers a way to meet like-minded people who have been through similar experiences and are on a journey to personal power. When women get together to share stories we can draw strength from one another and powerful growth can take place. If you are experiencing verbally, emotionally, sexually or physically destructive behaviour in your intimate relationship, attending a women's Living Without Violence support and education group can help to empower you. The following woman describes what being in one of these groups meant to her:

> Being in a support group has been a big part of my becoming stronger – just having somewhere to go where I could say what was really happening for me and know I wouldn't be judged. From my support group I get unquestioning, unconditional support and understanding and validation. It's amazing because I've found in myself stuff that I thought I'd lost a long time ago. When I look at other women I realise how far I have come and how well I'm doing. We're all at different stages but we're all on the same journey, striving for the same thing. We all want to come out the end feeling whole, happy and intact.

These groups can offer you practical information and assist you in assessing your situation and planning strategies that will help to keep you (and your children) safe. If you are being overpowered by a family member, an older child, or in the workplace, attending one of these groups may also be helpful. For information about a women's support group in your area phone the National Network of Stopping Violence Services (04 499 6384). This organisation will also be able to provide information about the men's Living Without Violence Programmes which offers help to men who are wanting to change controlling or abusive behaviours and build respectful relationships. Of course while we may suggest to someone they attend such a programme it is up to the person concerned if he is willing to take that step. Meanwhile it is vital we continue to focus on ourselves and ensure we get the help and information we need.

Use the Energy of Anger

The feeling of anger is a useful signal that something is wrong. It can alert us to the fact we are under threat: someone is overstepping the mark, pushing our boundaries and not respecting our rights. As women many of us have difficulty in acknowledging and expressing our anger. (See 'Women and Anger', p. 99.) We are more inclined to become angry on someone else's behalf rather than our own. If we have experienced ongoing bullying we may have lost – or never developed – the ability to express our anger at the injustices inflicted on us.

> *Even when I moved out of home my mother kept saying dreadful things about me to my girlfriends and the family. She even talked to my husband about me. He was very supportive. In fact he was outraged. That was the first time I'd experienced healthy outrage. Like, how could someone do that to me? That changed my perception. Before that I didn't have outrage. I was a real victim. I'd lost my ability to fight back. I'd been crushed. After that I began to stand up for myself.*

It may not always be appropriate or advisable to express anger directly if that would put our safety or livelihood at stake, but it is important we allow ourselves to know when we are angry. When we ignore our angry feelings we lose vital information that can help us to identify and clarify what is happening. We can also slip more easily into depression. Anger is a form of energy that provides the impetus for action.

Strategies for Harnessing Anger

▶ **Give yourself permission to feel your anger.** Anger is a healthy response to being hurt.

▶ **Listen to the message of your anger.** When you feel angry stop and ask yourself:
  – What is my anger telling me?
  – In what ways am I being hurt?
  – What do I need to do about it?

▶ **Focus the anger on the person who is doing the hurting.** You have every right to feel angry if someone is hurting you. It is important this anger is directed at the appropriate person, not innocent others or yourself. However, this doesn't mean you have to express it directly if you don't feel it is safe to do so.

▶ **Talk your anger through with someone you trust.** Expressing your anger is far more healthy than bottling it up.

▶ **Consider expressing your anger directly to the person concerned.** Try using the formula for assertive communication on p. 129.

▶ **If you are not able to express your anger directly find a safe outlet for it**. Anger can be released by writing or art or physical activity such as exercise, dancing, gardening or housework.

⬗ **Write an angry letter that you do not intend to send.** In this letter you can fully vent your emotions. Destroy the letter when you have finished.

Use Positive Self-talk

The messages we tell ourselves have an enormous impact on how we feel about ourselves and how confident we feel about dealing with power games. When we allow our sense of powerlessness to get the better of us we often give ourselves messages that reinforce and increase our distress. We can consciously choose to calm our fears and build our confidence by noticing and challenging our negative self-talk and telling ourselves things that strengthen us.

> I'm challenging the chatterbox in my head, the little voice that I've heard for years from my ex-husband, my family, my parents that tells me that I can't do it, that I'm not good enough. I'm saying now, 'Lies. I don't believe this any more,' and then I say positive things to myself about who I am, and that's empowering me too. I've got to reject these negative things to gain personal power.

When you are feeling doubtful or afraid try taking deep, slow breaths and repeating positive messages such as:

⬗ 'I have the power to protect myself.'
⬗ 'I deserve to be treated with respect.'
⬗ 'I believe in myself.'
⬗ 'I can stand up for myself.'
⬗ 'I have the right to express my ideas and opinions.'
⬗ 'My feelings and needs are important.'
⬗ 'I'm okay. I can handle this.'

While you may not believe these messages at first, just saying them to yourself can make you feel calmer and more in control. By consistently challenging self-defeating thoughts and repeating affirmations like these we will gradually replace old, limiting, fearful beliefs with empowering new ones.

Questions to Consider

▶ What negative labels do I put on myself?

▶ What fearful things do I tell myself about my ability to deal with power games?

▶ What can I tell myself that will help me to feel powerful and strong?

Make yourself a list of appropriate empowering messages. Commit several to memory and say them to yourself often.

Decide on a Course of Action

Whether destructive behaviour is taking place within a close relationship or the workplace or community it is important to take stock and decide what action to take. There are four general choices we can make when suffering within power games:

▶ We can accept the situation and attempt to live with it.

▶ We can quietly work at looking after ourselves, meanwhile making a plan and biding our time until we are ready to take action.

▶ We can decide to actively take a stand to protect ourselves and regain our power.

▶ We can get away from the power games by leaving a relationship, job or community.

Making a choice and acting on it takes us from powerlessness to empowerment. Having assessed our situation we may decide to continue on in this way for now. However, we have at least made a choice.

We can reassess and choose again when we are ready. We are already more in control of our situation.

Questions to Consider
▶ What are all the possible courses of action in this situation?
▶ What are the pros and cons of these possible actions?
▶ What is the best course of action for me at this time?
▶ How can I best look after myself?
▶ What support do I need to empower me to act?

Take a Stand
Taking a stand against a powerful person is a challenge, especially if we are worn out and afraid of conflict or retaliation. Taking a stand may mean:
▶ insisting on a lunch break to an overbearing boss;
▶ going to the gym despite a controlling partner's protests;
▶ saying no to the relative who would exploit our generosity;
▶ challenging a child's defiance and banning TV-watching as a consequence.

In a sense taking a stand against power games involves us in a power struggle: a struggle to claim back the power that is rightfully ours. When considering taking a stand we need to weigh our energy levels, confidence and resilience against the importance of the issue and potential gains to be made. When choosing between standing our ground and giving in it is important to be realistic about the effect that consistent capitulation has on us. As we have seen in Chapter 5 'The Impact of Power Games', when we continue to resort to powerlessness as a coping strategy we increasingly lose ground. At the same time we need to be realistic. Ideally we would take a stand only on those issues we feel at the time we can stand firm on. If we have already lost a lot of our power it is better to begin setting limits gradually, one at a time, starting with smaller issues and working up.

When we decide to set limits we need to prepare for the other person's resistance. He or she may escalate their power games when they sense they do not have the same control as they did before. We need to be prepared to ride this out. We may feel we are at the mercy of this person's moods and manipulations but it is possible to limit the effect of this to some extent. For example if we say no to sex and our partner retaliates by sulking angrily for days this will be unsettling and probably anxiety-provoking. There is little we can do to change the other person's behaviour. However, we do have some degree of choice about how much we are going to let this reaction upset us. We can decide to view this as yet another power game, refuse to be drawn into the drama and focus on looking after our self instead. It is important to decide in advance how we can best support ourselves through this tense time. Other people's encouragement will often help to sustain us.

When taking a stand the more prepared you are the more likely your success so take the time to create an action plan. Decide in advance what you will say and do. It can be helpful to go though the details of the plan with your support person and rehearse your part until you feel reasonably confident. Try to anticipate possible problems that would cause you to cave in and work out strategies to prevent this happening. If your action involves a face-to-face confrontation and you are feeling shaky about it consider taking your support person with you. There are many ways of getting your point across using varying degrees of directness. (See 'Become More Assertive', p. 129.) Here are some forthright examples:

Powerful Stand-taking Statements

- ▶ 'I don't agree when you say that.'
- ▶ 'That's your opinion, but I have a different one.'

▶ 'No, that's not okay for me.'

▶ 'No, I don't want to do that.'

▶ 'No, I'm not prepared to . . .'

▶ 'I'd prefer you to . . .'

▶ 'I am not willing to be treated this way.'

▶ 'I don't agree with what you are saying about me.'

▶ 'I'm not willing to discuss this subject at the moment.'

▶ 'If you don't stop putting me down I'm leaving the room.'

▶ 'I find your comments about me insulting.'

▶ 'I'm not prepared to discuss this while you're shouting.'

▶ 'I'm finding your behaviour offensive.'

Understandably some women feel too intimidated and worn down to take such a direct, assertive stand, but taking a stand does not necessarily need to involve the other person so directly. It can be any action that we take to strengthen ourselves in the situation. The first step may simply be to gain some time and space so you can think through your options.

> *I went to my doctor and got him to sign me off work for a week. I was so burnt out. During that time I did a lot of soul-searching and talking to friends and I realised things couldn't go on like this any more. Something had to change.*

We can regain our power slowly, step by step, gradually standing our ground on the bigger issues as we become more confident.

> *Learning to stand up for myself has been amazing. I used to just let people walk all over me, but not any more. I started to take charge of my life in small ways at first. I decided to stop apologising all the time for things that weren't my fault. Then I started saying no to overtime when I didn't want to stay. From there I progressed to setting other limits with my supervisor.*

When he got uptight I started to tell him there was no need for him to take his anger out on me, I was doing the best I could and it wasn't my fault if we couldn't make the deadline. One day he was really hassling me and I'd just had enough and I told him to get off my back, I was going as fast as I could and the work would get done when I got a chance to do it and not before. Amazingly, it worked and he backed off. It was like he realised that I'd had enough, and he respected that.

As we increasingly stand our ground the other person is likely to either begin to back off and respect our stance or increase their power games. If it's the latter we will eventually need to weigh up the facts and decide whether the situation is a viable one for us to remain in. Sometimes leaving is the best option (see p. 138). As distressing as it may be to consider leaving a relationship or job that is important to us, it is vital we make our well-being a priority.

Questions to Consider

▶ What small issue might I take a stand on?

▶ What are my greatest fears about taking a stand?

▶ Are these fears realistic?

▶ How can I prepare in advance for these possible difficulties?

▶ Can I foresee a positive outcome if I stand my ground?

▶ Will standing my ground put my safety at risk?

▶ Do I need to consider involving other people (e.g. a support person or friend, a supervisor, the human resources manager or personnel manager, a mediator, the union, a lawyer, the police)? See 'Community Resources' p. 272.

Make a list of about five steps you could take to regain your power over time. Begin gradually to work your way through your list.

Become More Assertive

Assertiveness techniques can offer us new ways of expressing ourselves that are likely to have other people take us seriously. When power games are being played and we express ourselves assertively we are moving from the powerlessness of silent, stewing submission to a position of personal power. We are saying boldly, yet respectfully, how it is for us. We are claiming our right to be treated with respect and letting the other person know when they have overstepped our boundaries. Here is one woman's description of what happened when she made the decision to become more assertive.

> *Instead of banging my head against a brick wall, I knew I had to do it another way. I decided the next time the bullying happened I would deal with it directly. I knew I had to do it well because it would just continue if I didn't, so I was on tenterhooks waiting for the time. When it came I actually stood back from the situation and said, 'This behaviour is unacceptable. I want you to stop it now. This is not the place for this.' After that it stopped because I'd actually cut through it. The overt, abusive, shouting tantrums did not happen again. The bullying did go underground in far more subtle ways but that really nasty stuff stopped so I felt as if I'd achieved something.*

A Four-part Formula for Making an Assertive Statement

1. Begin with describing the situation that is unacceptable.
2. Use an 'I' statement to describe your feelings.
3. State what you would like to happen instead.
4. Give the person a positive consequence of change (if appropriate) or state the consequence of the behaviour continuing.

For example:

1. When I receive this amount of work to do before I go home at night . . .
2. I feel overwhelmed.
3. It would be helpful if you would prioritise the most important tasks that can realistically be achieved by the end of the day.
4. That way I will get the work done that you need most urgently and still get to leave on time.

You can see from the example that the language of assertiveness is clear, direct, unemotional and non-blaming. In effect you are giving your feedback about inappropriate behaviour and the impact it is having on you and offering a suggestion for change that will provide a better outcome for you, and if possible for the other person too. Naming the behaviour in this way is empowering because it lets the other person know you recognise clearly what is happening and that you do not agree with it. The issue has been clearly defined and a possible solution suggested.

. When using this formula keep your statement as short, to the point and factual as possible. Focus on your own experience and speak for yourself, using 'I' statements that describe your experience. Avoid using 'you' statements as this usually comes across as accusing. Restrict your comments about the other person to their behaviour, not their personality or their possible motives.

The way you deliver the message is just as important as the content. As much as you are able stand tall and don't be apologetic or hesitant. Hold steady eye contact, keep your voice firm and your tone moderate. Remind yourself that you have the right to be treated with respect. Because this type of communication focuses primarily on your own experience it is difficult for the other person to invalidate what you are saying, provided you stay firmly with your experience and feelings.

These are your unique responses and as such they are valid. Remember, you don't have to justify why you feel as you do. When you have delivered your message leave it at that. If you are drawn into a debate or argument you may well begin to lose ground. If the person begins to question, argue or try to change your mind, repeat the brief assertive statement again without elaborating or making excuses, then disengage from the discussion.

As straightforward as this technique sounds it can of course be very challenging to use in real life when you are dealing with a person who is misusing power. Sometimes the other person is so committed to behaving destructively that your assertiveness will make little difference. Sometimes, however, the other person will listen to our feedback and begin to treat us more respectfully, perhaps because they are apprehensive about our new way of behaving and sense they no longer have the power over us that they did. Even if this doesn't happen, the advantage in using assertive communication is that at least you have gone on record clearly stating your feedback and expressing your feelings. This in itself is empowering and will probably make you feel better about yourself. As you become more assertive the contrast between your directness and the other person's style of communication may become blatantly obvious. This may help to clarify who is responsible for the problems and clear up any self-doubt and confusion you are experiencing.

Strategies for Setting Limits Assertively

▶ **Take time to decide on which issue to tackle first.**
Which issue is most important? Choose something small to begin with.

▶ **Listen to your feelings and body reactions** and use these as a guide:
– Do you get that sinking feeling in your stomach at the

prospect of doing what the other person wants?

– What is it you need to say?

▶ **Clarify which of your rights is being violated.** If you are
   not sure check with the list of rights on p. 270.

▶ **Decide what your limits are.** Ask yourself:

   – What do I want in this situation?

   – What am I not willing to tolerate any more?

▶ **Plan what you want to say** using the formula above. Write
   it out and practise it first to build your clarity and confidence.

▶ **When delivering your message choose your own time
   and place if possible.**

▶ **You do not have to give reasons or justifications for
   what you are saying.** You have the right to decide what is
   best for you and to clearly state that.

▶ **Keep to your point.** Refuse to let yourself be manipulated by
   blaming, hostile silence, guilt trips, badgering, threats and/or
   anger.

▶ **Refuse to feel guilty.** You do not have to be all things to all
   people. It is important that you take care of your needs and
   claim your rights.

Keep Yourself Safe

Beware of taking a stand if it is likely to result in violence against you.
Never compromise your safety for the sake of making a direct stand. It's not
worth it. There are other indirect actions you can take to empower
yourself, such as disclosing what is happening to other people and
enlisting their support (see 'Build Your Support' p. 119).

   If you are suffering from any form of physical abuse or are afraid
for your safety you need to seriously consider your options. Usually
when power games have reached this stage they are part of an
escalating pattern which becomes increasingly undermining and

dangerous. *You don't deserve to be mistreated. No-one has the right to physically abuse you.*

If you are living with a person who is physically abusive, at the very least it is important to have an escape plan worked out. Decide ahead of time what you would do if you needed to leave. Who would you call on for help? Where would you go? How would you get there? Work through the possibilities with a counsellor or your support person. Arrange for friends, family or neighbours to help you in a crisis. Consider also having someone else talk to the person concerned about the inappropriateness of his or her behaviour. Keep the phone numbers of helping agencies on hand and spare keys, important documents, essential medication and a change of clothes accessible in case you need to leave in a hurry. If the person becomes threatening make an excuse to leave the house. It can also be a good idea to seek legal assistance and take out a protection order. Seriously consider involving the police if a threatening incident occurs.

If you are being harassed by someone close to you, going to stay in a safe, confidential place can be the best option. A women's refuge or shelter offers information, advice, assistance and accommodation for women who are in physically or emotionally threatening situations. They provide a wonderful supportive service to women from all walks of life. (See 'Community Resources' p. 272 for further information.)

Going into a women's refuge meant peace, and freedom from all the fear. It was an amazing experience. There were so many women of different nationalities but we were all there for the same reasons at the end of the day and the women were incredible. The day after I went in I was sitting there crying and this Chinese woman with a story even worse than mine came up to me and gave me a hug and I just felt this sense that she knew what I was going through, she understood, and after everything she had been through she still had something to give me. It was there I had the realisation that

there was something to live for, and that together we could all get
through it.

Dealing with Power Games in the Workplace

The strategies already covered in this chapter are obviously applicable to dealing with workplace power games as well as those in close relationships. In addition there are some extra strategies you can use if you are experiencing destructive behaviour in the workplace.

When the pressure is on it is easy to begin to neglect our needs, skip breaks and focus our dwindling energy on just getting by. This can compound our problems by pushing us towards burnout. *It is vital that we do all we can to care for ourselves and make our day-to-day situation more bearable.* You are entitled to your lunch break so don't let pressure from a demanding boss stop you. Make the most of your break by arranging to meet a friend for lunch, going for a brisk walk, going window shopping or to your favourite restaurant, catching up with colleagues, reading an inspirational book, writing in your journal or finding a quiet place to relax. Even small touches like taking flowers to your office or sending funny e-mails to your colleagues can help to lighten your spirits. As much as possible keep a balance in your life. Take regular exercise, eat a healthy diet and maintain interests and friends outside work.

Having strong alliances with colleagues usually helps us to feel more powerful. Colleagues can provide us with moral support, offer survival strategies and provide us with a reality check about the bullying we are experiencing. It can be a good idea to arrange to get together outside the workplace so people have the opportunity to share honestly about work experiences, let off steam and plan strategies. Realising that other people have similar concerns can be enormously validating. Together it can be possible to take a stand against power games that it would be too risky or daunting to face alone.

Other Workplace Strategies

▶ **Keep a detailed written record of each incident** of bullying (however minor) including dates, times, and any witnesses. Make sure it is factual.

▶ **Keep copies of all relevant documents** including job descriptions, written instructions, appraisals and letters concerning your work.

▶ **Request written instructions** if verbal instructions are unclear.

▶ **Avoid being alone with the person** who is being destructive as much as possible.

▶ **Check the limits of your job description** to make sure you are not being expected to work outside it.

▶ **Gain support** from outside the workplace.

▶ **Ask for feedback about your work** from colleagues you respect and trust if you have self-doubts.

▶ **Establish what the complaint procedures** are within your organisation.

▶ **Consider gaining input from a counsellor** either at your workplace or in the community.

▶ **Confide in your doctor** about what is happening if stress is affecting your work performance. It may be appropriate to get a medical certificate to allow you time off work to regain your strength and reassess your situation.

▶ **Try making an assertive response** when the bullying occurs if you feel strong enough.

▶ **Consider joining an assertiveness course** to gain practical strategies and encouragement.

▶ **Consider making a complaint** to the person above the bullying person, the manager of human resources or the personnel manager if you have one.

    ❱ **Consider approaching your union, a mediation service or the Human Rights Commission for assistance.**

Strategies for Dealing with Sexual Harassment

As we have discussed, sexual harassment in the workplace is unacceptable and it is also illegal, and we do not have to put up with it. There are a number of specific actions we can take to deal with this form of bullying:

    ❱ **Tell the person clearly that you find his or her behaviour inappropriate and offensive and ask them to stop.** Be sure that your body language and manner reflect your firmness in this.

    ❱ **Keep a written record of each incident** and a copy of all relevant written material.

    ❱ **Consider reporting the incident/s to a supervisor or employer.**

    ❱ **Put your well-being ahead of the harasser's.** Protect yourself, not the other person. He or she is responsible for their own actions.

    ❱ **Give the person a pamphlet on sexual harassment**, either silently or with the information that you will not tolerate sexual harassment and you will take it further if he or she doesn't stop.

    ❱ **Write a letter to the person**, giving a factual account of what happened including the date, time and place and how the incident affected you. Date the letter and write 'Personal and Confidential' on the top. Also write this on the outside of the envelope and seal it. Keep a copy.

    ❱ **Confront the person face to face.** This needs to be done out of the hearing of others to avoid accusations of defamation. You may wish to be in public view however for you own protection.

▶ **Challenge the person directly when the inappropriate behaviour is happening** if you feel strong enough. Try using the formula for making an assertive statement outlined on p. 129. Don't feel you have to discuss the issue further. Just deliver your message, turn around and leave.

▶ **Consider making direct statements:**
'Leave me alone.'
'I find that offensive.'
'I object to you treating me like that.'
'You have no right to do that.'
'If you don't stop that I'm going to take further action.'

▶ **Seek the support of appropriate people.** The people who have a right to know may include your supervisor or employer, a counsellor, your union representative or a mediator. If you do not get a respectful and supportive hearing from one person try someone else.

▶ **Be careful who you talk to informally.** The accused person can claim defamation of character if you name him or her publicly and make accusations that are likely to injure his or her reputation.

▶ **Consider making a complaint through formal channels** such as a mediator or a lawyer if other strategies have not worked. They will advise and take action on your behalf if there are suitable grounds. (See 'Community Resources, p. 272.)

Sometimes Breaking Contact Is the Best Option

When we are experiencing power games many of us pour endless amounts of energy into trying to improve the situation. If our efforts continue to far outweigh any rewards by way of positive changes, our commitment and persistence can become self-defeating.

When a relationship is fixed in an overwhelmingly negative pattern stepping away from it, at least for a time, may be the only way we can gain any peace of mind.

> *Divorcing Mum is the most sensible thing I've done because I had to break that tie with her, I had to get away from her. I've got to make my own life. If I didn't then I think I could become a very bitter and angry person because I'll always have that fighting relationship with her and that will hold me back. Her verbal abuse is just mindless words that go round and round like a broken record and all it did was to strip two people of their dignity and self-respect. It just injured and continually undermined. When I started to see the wider picture I thought, 'This is just a load of crap. There's no point in it. I don't need this in my life any more.'*

Sometimes a temporary break in a relationship allows space for issues to be faced honestly and positive changes to take place. Obviously breaking contact with someone who is important to us is a decision not to be taken lightly but if we are still being mistreated even after our best efforts to resolve the difficulties in the relationship and set healthy boundaries this kind of last resort may eventually be necessary.

Sometimes the best option is to break contact permanently. *Deciding to leave a situation that is proving destructive is an act of power.* In choosing to leave we are affirming that we are important and declaring that we will not continue to waste our energy in a situation that is going nowhere. We do have the strength to rebuild again. When we finally say 'enough' we at least emerge with our self-respect.

> *At the end of the day I realised I had no future there in terms of my professional career, so I made the choice to leave that unhealthy*

environment and leave my career behind. I was not going to be able
to achieve anything else and it would have been to my detriment
to keep trying. I decided to make a deliberate transition into
another career. It was sad for me because that was my first love and
I had a huge investment in my career. It took me about two years
to get out, to come to terms with having to leave and then to be
quite clear that the choice I was making wasn't about leaving. It
was about going forward to something else. It was a high personal
cost to me but it's funny, because if that hadn't happened I
wouldn't be in the position I'm in today, which is far more
satisfying and lucrative than my other career ever would have
been. I struggled with it at the time but it has worked out well.

In deciding whether and when to give up and walk away it is important to remember that the longer we hang in there with escalating power games the less confidence, clarity and energy we will have to make the final decision and take action.

Giving up on a relationship or job to which we have given our time, commitment, energy and emotional input is a huge decision. Often the more we have given the harder it can be to cut our losses and leave. But it is important to count honestly the personal cost of our efforts and ask ourselves what we are gaining from sacrificing our well-being in this way. We don't need to settle for being worn down, hurt and dominated. There are other jobs and other people to share our time with – people who will appreciate our efforts and treat us with the respect we are entitled to.

One of the most important things about leaving is that we take responsibility for the decision we are making. If we leave in a powerless way, saying, 'I had no choice,' then it will be more difficult to pick up the pieces. But if we declare, 'I wasn't prepared to put up with being mistreated any longer,' we are in a much stronger position.

Questions to Consider

▶ Have you tried all the strategies you want to try to challenge the situation?

▶ Is the other person willing to admit to having a problem with using hurtful behaviour and seek help to make changes?

▶ What is staying in this situation costing you emotionally, mentally and physically?

▶ Overall is the situation improving or deteriorating?

▶ If the situation continues as it is, how do you see yourself coping six months, one year and five years from now?

▶ Is the cost worth it?

▶ If you are not ready to give up yet what will your bottom line be? What will signal to you that it is time to leave?

Move Beyond the Pain of the Past

Obviously when we leave a person or a job that has been important to us it will take time to come to terms with this and we will grieve. Grieving is a natural process that accompanies any significant change, even a positive one. This is because all change brings with it losses as well as gains. The best way to get out of grief is to move through it, to allow ourselves the sadness and tears, denial and bargaining, anger and outrage, regret and yearning. These emotions gradually pave the path to acceptance of our loss and new-found confidence and strength.

If we have often been on the receiving end of other people's destructive power as a child or as an adult, we can be left with an ongoing sense of helplessness and powerlessness and the belief that we do not have control over our own life. Leaving these feelings and beliefs behind begins with the bold decision to claim personal power and continues with a gradual process of self-discovery, healing and practising new skills.

I've been able to develop the necessary tools to not be a victim any more and that's what it's all about. In my experience when I was in victim mode I tended to stay there. I'd cry at the drop of a hat and wouldn't assert myself at all. As a victim I didn't have to be responsible for me. Everyone else would take care of me, this poor little sad waif. Then it got to a point last year when I thought, 'I don't want to be like this any more. I want to be in control of my own life. I want to have power inside myself.' That was a turning point and after that things began to change for the better. Now I feel much stronger in myself. I now only have people in my life who are not abusive and if anyone tries to bully me I move away from them.

If we have been badly hurt the important thing is that we find our own way to honestly work through what has happened. (See 'Healing Past Hurts' p. 233.) Sometimes confronting the destructive person and letting him or her know how hurtful their behaviour has been can be an important way of reclaiming our power and resolving some of the conflicted emotions we feel. This is usually a hugely challenging step to take. Deciding whether and when to confront someone who has hurt us is a personal choice that needs to be made carefully in our own time. It is not necessary to confront the person in order to heal. Many women never directly confront the person but find other ways of dealing with the situation such as therapy, ritual, art work or letter writing. For other women speaking directly to the person about their distressing experience can be freeing and empowering.

The other day I thought about my mother and for the first time I thought, 'You've got no power over me.' That has a lot to do with the fact that I've confronted her with everything. I told her I loved her but I'd never forget what she'd done. I wasn't angry. I didn't swear at her or lash out at her but I just knew that I needed to tell her how deeply I feel about what she'd done to me. There was no anger or hatred. It was like I'd gone past a barrier. I wasn't blaming myself for saying those things. I had to do it to heal my little girl inside who was still hurting like shit and saying, 'Mummy you've hurt me.'

If you decide to confront it is essential to feel strong and ready within yourself. Be clear about what you need to say. It is important to do the confrontation for yourself as a way of getting it out of your system and putting the record straight. Don't expect a good reception from the person who has hurt you. It is likely that he or she will respond in their usual manner rather than with the reassurances or remorse you may long for. Don't underestimate the destructive power that person's behaviour may still have to upset you and throw you off balance. Consider taking a support person with you. It is much better not to confront at all or wait until you feel strong enough to take that step successfully than to act too quickly and come away feeling you have been wounded yet again. Never put your safety at risk.

Finding Spiritual Strength

I hate to think what would have happened to me if I hadn't faced fearful things with God, keeping in with Him all the way. At times I've been absolutely devastated, but my faith has just seen me through. It's like I've been pulled through again and again. That's why I've got such faith, because God has always been there. I've survived. Sometimes I look back and I wonder how.

Each of us has our own individual, personal beliefs about spirituality. Many of us hold a concept of a higher power which we relate to and rely on to provide support and strength in the good times and the bad and this can be enormously comforting and empowering.

This chapter has offered many possible strategies that can help you to regain your sense of power when it has been diminished by someone's power games. Although we can not control other people's behaviour we can take care of ourselves, seek the help we need, decide on a course of action, begin to stand up for ourselves (when appropriate and safe) and protect ourselves if necessary. It can take time to deal with other people's destructive behaviour but it is certainly possible if we persist. Each of us will gradually find the strategies to use that are most helpful and sustaining for us.

PART THREE

WHEN WE USE POWER GAMES AGAINST OTHERS

CHAPTER 8

The Ways We Hurt the Ones We Are Close to

I t is those we are closest to – our partners, children, parents, relatives and close friends – who are most likely to bear the brunt of our hurtful power. Yet these are the very people with whom we usually want to build happy, sustaining relationships. Those we are closest to trigger our most intense emotions: neediness, desperation, hurt, rejection, jealousy, fear, anger and vindictiveness. These emotions can translate into an overriding need to get our own way, take control or pay the other person back for a perceived injustice or hurt. We can become so intent on 'winning' we lose sight of the harm we are doing – not only to the other person but also to our self.

It is not usually the minor occasional hurtful episodes that harm people. The real harm is done when we continue to undermine someone's self-esteem and put pressure on them to submit to our wishes regardless of what they themselves want.

Facing up to the fact that we are hurting people with our power takes courage. The social stigma against women who act in harmful ways is a strong deterrent to women speaking out. In this chapter women do speak out – with honesty and regret – about those times in

their lives when they inflicted pain on the people they were close
to. As we have already seen in Chapter 2 'Being Hurt in Close Relationships' there are numerous ways to undermine a person we are
close to.

Overstepping Others' Limits

*I dominated my kids as they grew up. I meant well but I tried to
take over their lives. I had no faith in them. Whatever they wanted
to do I had a hundred reasons why not. When I look back I can see
I was really pushy. I'd question and lecture them and imply they
were stupid if they saw things differently to me. If they wanted to
go against what I was saying I'd become really nasty and argue
them down. Most of the time they just shut down and went along
with things. I think they were really quite scared of my disapproval. Somehow it never occurred to me for a long time that I was
being quite bullying.*

It is easy to overlook other people's right to have privacy, make their
own decisions, make their own mistakes and refuse help. This is especially true with the people we care about. We may have the best of
intentions as we insist on trying to solve other people's problems for
them, but if this is done in a disrespectful, controlling way then we are
overstepping the limits. We are being overbearing when we foist
unsolicited advice on people, interrogate them, invade their privacy and
try to take over their lives while ignoring their protests. We are being
punishing when we use sulking, anger, criticism, sarcasm or other
means to pay that person back for non-compliance with our wishes.

Manipulation

*I was always power-tripping my partners. I knew how to get my
own way: how far I could push and, if I didn't get what I wanted,*

> *how to make someone feel bad. It was a selfish thing. When things were not going too well I'd say to my partner, 'I'm going to catch up with Claire, my ex-partner,' and she'd know what I was doing. It was a power trip to make her say, 'Don't go,' to get her back in the cycle of fear and insecurity. No matter what she said I'd say the opposite. I'd tell her I was leaving if she wanted me to stay, but if she told me to go, I'd refuse.*

We are using emotional manipulation when we find ways to manoeuvre other people into doing what we want by evoking and playing on their feelings of compassion, obligation, guilt or anxiety. Sometimes we may be so caught up in our own needs we fail to recognise the bind we are putting the other person into. At other times we may be quite aware that we are using this strategy to achieve our own ends.

> *I was very good at playing games. My friend was in a relationship with a guy and I was jealous, so I painted a black picture of him to her. That was my way of wrecking it for her so that I wouldn't lose her. I did it consciously. I knew that it would upset her and she'd come to me for someone to talk to and console her. I knew that if I did that she'd need me.*

Mind Games

> *I used to get Marie really confused because I'd make up anything that suited me. I'd always twist things around so that I was the innocent one and she was the bad one. Like I'd be late, so I'd change the time we arranged to meet and tell her she had it wrong. She'd try to argue back but I'd just shut her down by getting angry.*

There are many ways of deliberately creating confusion in another person. We can deny things, distort the facts, contradict ourselves and blame. When the other person tries to put the record straight we can dismiss or out-argue them, put them down or accuse them of being wrong or lying. Our adamant version of 'reality' may be so convincing that over time the other person begins to think he or she is crazy.

The Silent Treatment

If I didn't get my own way I wouldn't speak to Simon – not a word. I'd completely and utterly shut down. He used to try and go through the kids: 'Ask your mother if she wants some dinner.' But I'd think, 'This is my way of teaching you that I have control of this situation. I will talk when I want to, not when you want me to.'

Ignoring someone can be a powerful means of punishing them for not doing what we want or pressuring them to conform. Since most people find it painful to be ignored it is likely that the other person will soon try to 'make up'. While using the silent treatment we will often be justifying our position by telling ourselves the other person is to blame. Consequently our withdrawal is usually accompanied by smouldering anger. This can add to the other person's feelings of distress and anxiety.

Emotional Wounding

There have been times when I've gone right off at my children. Sometimes they make me so furious I just hate them. Sometimes I feel so trapped by them, always there, always wanting things. It just drives me up the wall. When I really lose it I stand over them and scream my head off. I lash out and call them everything I can think of. I just want them to be sorry.

Our words have enormous power to wound those we are close to. We can use words to discredit and attack their worth, motives and ideas and make them feel inadequate and ashamed. Sometimes we can make subtle digs, barbed comments, criticisms and put-downs without thinking of the effect on the other person's confidence. Sometimes we just don't care.

> *I'd say things to Kevin like, 'You're nothing but a useless bastard.'*
> *I said that so often that he actually thought he was. He took the*
> *blame on and thought, 'Maybe it is me.' Sometimes he was so hurt*
> *with the horrible things I'd said it would take him weeks to get*
> *over it.*

Pushing the Limits

> *During the first six months I was so well behaved, put on the best*
> *show you'd ever seen. I didn't show my true colours because I*
> *wanted Peter so much. But I knew the aggressor in me had to come*
> *out sooner or later. I was just biding my time. We moved in*
> *together and then I started back into the old habits, telling him*
> *what to do and when and how to do it. Threatening him: 'You do it*
> *my way or else.' Peter wondered what the hell had struck him.*
> *How could a person that was so calm and cool and wonderful for a*
> *period of six months turn into a raging, out-of-control volcano? He*
> *was so shocked. He didn't know how to handle me. He was so*
> *confused he cried, often cried. He was just devastated.*

Most of us have a fair idea of what we can get away with. Obviously people who do not know us well and do not have a commitment to us are unlikely to stay around if we repeatedly hurt them. Those who have an emotional attachment to us are a different story. These people are very likely to put up with more, forgive our distressing blow-ups and give us many chances. This can seem to make them a safe and ready target on which to take out our frustrations.

Within the privacy of our close relationships we may feel free to act badly while showing a charming face to the rest of the world. Even when we have an 'uncontrollable' outburst we may be very selective about where and when this takes place. Our changeable behaviour can evoke feelings of insecurity and dependency in those we are close to. This is quite understandable. We hold enormous power over their well-being. Just as we can undermine their confidence on a whim we can also restore it by becoming remorseful, turning on the charm and promising never to do it again.

Once we have begun to get away with destructive behaviour in a particular relationship we may be lulled into a false sense of security. The highly charged emotions, stormy bust-ups and passionate make-ups can seem to bind us closely together. Intense feelings can be evoked in both parties: fear, anger, desperation and rejection. We may mistake this emotional intensity for love, especially in an intimate relationship. In the midst of the drama it is easy to overlook the fact that most people have a breaking point. There will very likely come a time when even the most tolerant, long-suffering, forgiving person will say, 'Enough!'

Insecure Accusations

I need John so much but I know I'm driving him away. I just want everything to be so good. If he seems a bit distant I start to panic. Then I hassle him. 'What's wrong? I know something's wrong. Tell me, I need to know.' He'll say, 'There's nothing wrong,' and try to get me to stop but I won't when I'm in that mood. I go on and on about it. I can see him getting upset and withdrawing but that just makes me worse. I get really angry and start to think he doesn't care about me. Then I become even louder and start to accuse him of not loving me or of wanting someone else. Sometimes I go as far as threatening to leave, even though this is the last thing I'd do. That really upsets him.

If we are insecure and needy we may put considerable pressure on someone close by becoming demanding and possessive. However, we are unlikely to get the reassurance and closeness we are looking for when we resort to using these methods. Usually the stronger we come on, the more distant and elusive the other person becomes. This can trigger more fear and desperation in us and so it becomes a vicious cycle.

Harassment and Intimidation

I just constantly gave Michael a hard time. I'd ring him at work and hound him on the phone. Here he was trying to do his job and I was on the other end of the phone telling him this and telling him that. At home everything had to be in its place, not a speck of dust was allowed to land on anything and if Michael moved the wrong way or sat the wrong way I'd just go at him. He'd do something as simple as leaving a knife in the sink and I'd just hit the roof: 'How dare you do this? Who do you think you are, leaving this for me to do?' He'd go and clean up but I could tell by the look on his face that he was really hurting.

When we resort to using standover tactics we generate fear in the other person. This ensures we are likely to get our own way – at least in that moment. As controlling behaviour usually escalates, intimidation and threats are often only a short step from physical abuse.

When I'd been mean to my daughter and she got upset it used to make me absolutely furious. 'What are you crying about? What's wrong with you? Don't be so pathetic. Shut up or I'll give you something to cry about.' Sometimes she'd just cry all the more then, but if I was really mad she'd do her best to stop crying. She was too scared to cry because she knew I'd really lose my cool.

Physical Abuse

> *I was really upset one day and I remember just crashing the lid of the van down on Colin's head, without even stopping to think about it. Fortunately he was wearing a hat at the time or I could have killed him. And I remember when I did it just being struck with horror. It was like a sick feeling. I thought, 'I've really done it now,' and I looked at his face and knew I'd pushed him too far. I pretended that I didn't realise what I'd done but he said to me, 'I'm leaving you.' I started to cry and said I was sorry, and he said, 'No, there's been too many incidents like this. I'm not strong enough for you.'*

If we have got to the stage of using any kind of physical abuse – including pushing, hitting, hair-pulling, kicking or slapping – we need to take this very seriously. Violence will surely destroy whatever trust and goodwill are left in the relationship and may also result in physical injuries to the other person.

> *Derek came home late one night and I flew at him and punched and punched and punched him. He just stood there and didn't even try to defend himself and then he just turned around and walked out and I remember screaming at him, 'Where do you think you're going?'*

Once a pattern of physical abuse has begun it is likely to escalate unless you find a way to stop, pull back and calm down. Chapter 12 'Choosing to Change' looks at a number of strategies that can help. If anyone is in physical danger you also need to seek immediate professional assistance.

Exercise: Acknowledge the Ways You Are Hurting Those You Are Close To

The one consistent theme of most power games is blame. *Blaming other people locks us into a place of powerlessness.* Unless we are willing to take responsibility for our hurtful behaviour we are likely to remain stuck in the illusion that other people are to blame for our bullying. From this place we have nowhere to go and no reason to change. We cling desperately to denial in the hope that we will prove to be the innocent party and be spared the pain of facing ourselves. The importance of moving out of denial is apparent in the following woman's experience.

> *I first of all had to see the ways I was dumping on people. I'd always seen the bullying in other people but I never saw it in myself. It was only when I allowed myself to see what I was doing that I could deal with it and make changes. What stopped me from seeing it in myself sooner was a lack of self-esteem, a lack of self-worth. That stopped me from looking honestly at the darkness I had inside and accepting it.*

Taking responsibility creates the possibility of change. *Although facing your destructive behaviour may be painful it will also increase your sense of personal power.* When you acknowledge you have a problem you open yourself up to finding ways to resolve the conflict in your relationships.

To take stock of the ways you are misusing your power complete the following list. Check (✔) each statement you identify with and define how true this is for you by choosing between the options. Place a question mark (?) beside those that are partially true for you.

_____ I know my manner towards someone close is often overbearing.

_____ I sometimes/often use guilt trips and emotional blackmail as a way of getting what I want.

_____ I sometimes/often use sarcasm, put-downs and verbal abuse.

_____ I sometimes/often push past others' 'no'.

_____ I sometimes/often play the 'poor me' game to manipulate others into doing what I want.

_____ I sometimes/often assume too much control over someone's life.

_____ I sometimes/often blame others for conflict rather than take responsibility for my controlling behaviour.

_____ I sometimes/often demand more attention, time and energy than the other person wants to give, or than I give them.

_____ I sometimes/often deliberately play mind games that leave others feeling confused.

_____ I sometimes/often use the silent treatment as a way of punishing/manipulating the other person.

_____ I feel justified in applying pressure when the other person does not do what I want.

_____ I often pretend to be 'nice' in front of other people but use power games behind closed doors.

_____ I sometimes/often deliberately frighten the other person as a way of gaining control.

_____ I have resorted to using physical violence.

It is important to use this process of facing up to destructive behaviour as a positive motivation for change. It is natural to have feelings of guilt if you have hurt another person but taking responsibility is not about beating yourself up, it is about looking to the future and resolving to do better next time.

As you have read this chapter and worked through the checklist you may have experienced many emotions. For some women facing the truth about their behaviour is a relief, for many others it can be a shock. If you are feeling distressed or overwhelmed it is important to find a safe outlet for these feelings. You may want to talk to your support person or write in your journal or go for a long walk or a run or have a soak in the bath while you reflect on the issues this chapter has raised for you.

CHAPTER 9

The Ways We Hurt Others at Work

Many of us behave hurtfully in the workplace sometimes – at least in minor ways. Sometimes we are so caught up in having our say or getting what we want that we can insensitively trample on someone's feelings. While pushing to get our own way we are unaware of the distress we are causing others. Under pressure most of us will become impatient, intolerant and short-tempered and perhaps take this out on others at times. However, these relatively minor isolated incidents do not in themselves necessarily qualify as power games. We cross the line into power games when we deliberately use our power to demean, undermine, manipulate or bully.

Any one of us can use power games at work, whether or not we have any real authority over the person we are targeting. If we are placed in the role of supervisor, boss or employer we may be more at risk of misusing power. In the hierarchy we automatically hold a degree of legitimate power over those beneath us and with this role comes the expectation that we will 'get the job done' reasonably efficiently. This can be a real challenge, especially when it comes to dealing effectively with others' inconsistencies or mistakes. It can be tempting to resort to using power games to get others to do what we want – quickly. But although this may produce short-term results the cost is high. Ongoing power games create resentment, apathy and opposition. Enthusiasm, goodwill and creativity are lost. Over time the worker or colleague is likely to begin to quietly resist our control. It can then take more and more force to achieve the same amount of compliance, resulting in increasing pain for all concerned.

There are numerous opportunities in the workplace to take our frustrations out on others if we feel so inclined. In this chapter women speak honestly about the ways they have hurt people at work.

Subtle Undermining

> *A lot of the time I just refused to even look at June. I'd just turn my back on her or give her a one-word answer. When I did speak I'd be offhand or I'd often talk over her or interrupt her or talk down to her like she didn't know anything. Sometimes I was quite sharp in the way I spoke. That was enough to give her the message.*

It is possible to make a person feel uncomfortable or demeaned in very subtle ways. A slightly scathing tone, sneering look, dismissive attitude or rejecting body language can cause the other person to shrivel inside. A condescending manner usually makes them feel inadequate and small. Sometimes we may be unaware of what we are doing and why. At other times we may take a dislike to someone and consciously set about bringing them down.

> *This woman at work reminded me of my sister and I've never got on with her. Everything she did rubbed me up the wrong way. I couldn't stand being around her. She'd try to speak to me and be friendly and I'd just cut her dead.*

When a person reminds us of someone we have had previous difficulties with we can begin to project our old experiences and expectations onto them. We can lose sight of who this person really is and imagine they have negative behaviours, characteristics and motives that do not belong to them. We may then begin to treat them unfairly. Sometimes we may not even be aware of what is triggering our reaction until we stop and think carefully about it.

Intolerance and Criticism

It drives me up the wall when people make mistakes and this office girl was always getting things wrong so I started to pick on her. I'd criticise her for the slightest little thing – really gave her a hard time. I watched her like a hawk and double-checked everything she did. I was determined to catch her out so I'd often interrogate her about what she was doing and why. When she did make a mistake I made sure the whole office knew about it. Eventually she couldn't take it any more and she left. Now I see that she was young and what she needed was support and extra training, not hounding.

Constant criticism destroys confidence and self-esteem. If we put enough pressure on someone they are likely to become increasingly fearful of making mistakes and incurring our wrath. Their perform- ance will usually deteriorate accordingly. As this is usually the opposite of what we are trying to achieve, it highlights our need to improve our interpersonal skills.

Sometimes we may deliberately want to create conflict. We may be feeling angry and wound up and want the release of a blow-up, so we become critical and demanding. Regardless of the other person's attempts to please us we are determined to find fault. We may skilfully manoeuvre them into the position of being 'wrong' so we have the excuse we are looking for to become hurtful.

Competition and Jealousy

> *There was a woman manager at work that nobody liked. She was
> one of us and then she was promoted and that was it. The word
> went out that it had gone to her head, that she was 'up herself' and
> thought she was great. After that we gave her such a hard time.
> We wouldn't speak to her or sit with her in the lunchroom. She
> would ask us to do something and even though we wouldn't openly
> defy her, we'd go as slowly as we could. We talked about her behind
> her back and called her 'the dragon' and often made quite nasty
> jokes about her. At the time it seemed funny but really it wasn't.
> In a way she became the scapegoat for all our frustrations on the
> job. The management were giving us a hard time but we had some-
> one to take it out on. Really, we made the poor woman's life
> hell.*

It is not uncommon to find women criticising other women without
mercy, attempting to bring them down, responding begrudgingly or
with indignation or open resentment towards women who are perceived as successful. Within a group setting or individually we may
wound other women by withholding support, making sniping comments, gossiping and using cutting sarcasm, harsh judgements and
underground hostility. We may habitually compare ourselves, our
homes, partners, children, bodies, possessions and all manner of
things. If we convince ourselves that we are better than certain other
people it can be a short step to treating these others disrespectfully. We
may also resort to jealously attacking other women we perceive as
being better than ourselves.

> *A new woman came to work and I really hated her. She was
> younger than me and single and had nice clothes and all the guys
> liked her. Suddenly it felt like I was just in the shadows and what I
> thought didn't matter. This bright young thing thought she knew*

everything and the way the guys went on they seemed to think so too. I got so fed up with her I really wanted to take her down a peg or two. I did everything I could to show her in a bad light. I didn't pass on messages, talked about her behind her back to everyone and I even went so far as to hide some important paperwork on a Friday afternoon. The whole office went into an uproar and blamed her. She ended up in tears.

Taking Frustration Out on Others

There were many times when I brought my personal hassles into work. Things at home were really grim. I was worried sick and wasn't sleeping well. I didn't have anyone to talk to so I'd bottle up all my frustrations and anger and dump them on my staff. I became quite a tyrant, criticising, complaining, demanding the impossible and blaming the staff when they couldn't come up with the goods. I made their life hell. Somehow that gave me a perverse sense of satisfaction. If my life was falling apart then why should they be happy and smiling?

If we are feeling unhappy in our personal relationships our distress and frustration can spill over into the workplace. We may try to compensate for our sense of powerlessness at home by dominating the people we work with. The fleeting relief that this may bring is offset by the lack of support we receive as a result of our harshness.

Slave-driving

I look back now at my time as supervisor and I can see that I was horrendous to work for. I was really arrogant. I used to give them a really hard time and be really scathing. I thought I was better than all the other women. I was younger, better groomed, more switched on, I worked harder and achieved more. I thought I was really great. I hate to think now how I came across. I really thought I was so important. In a way I think it was a case of moving too far, too fast. I just got so into the power after I was promoted. It was really heady.

There is some truth in the old saying that power corrupts. We obtain legitimate power over others when we are placed in a supervisory position. But with this power comes the responsibility to be considerate, respectful and humane. Effective management consists of finding ways to work alongside those we manage in order to achieve a common goal. When we use our power in an overbearing way we can make others anxious and panicky. Under this kind of pressure mistakes are often made and absenteeism and staff turnover can be high.

I treated my secretary like a machine. If things weren't done on time I'd fly off the handle and demand she stayed late, even though she had a family to get home to. I was often nasty and rude to her. If there was a mistake in her typing I'd be scathing and demand she redo it in her own time. After a while I could see that she was losing ground. She became really apologetic and tried harder and harder to please, but this just fanned my fury.

Using Blame to Silence Others

I always blamed everyone else for everything that happened that made me angry. I didn't want to admit I needed help. I guess it was pride. I thought people would use it to their advantage. It seemed easier to pretend that I was in charge and right than to face other people looking down on me. If anyone even dared to hint at the fact that I had a problem I'd just go off my face at them. Whenever anything went wrong at work I'd make sure I came on so strong

about it that no-one dared to challenge me, even when I knew
damned well that it was my fault.

We may be quite well aware of how destructive we are being, yet fear others giving us this feedback. We refuse to listen to or accept the truth because if we acknowledge the truth we are afraid we will have to do something about it. We prefer to create a smokescreen of blame and accusations. If we can make enough noise and create enough confusion we can keep the focus off ourselves. Our persistent denial keeps us stuck, and often the more stuck we become the more we lash out at those around us.

Intimidation

I was always aggressive at work to the point where people were
frightened of me. They were scared of my wrath. I even had my
boss tell me that. They were actually too scared to ask me for help
because they thought I'd go right off at them. I had one really bad
barney at work where I screamed and shouted but mostly it was
just me giving people a hard time. Everything would go along
smoothly for a while and I'd just bottle things up instead of dealing
with them and sorting them out. Then I'd explode and anyone
who got in my way would just cop it in a huge way. I'd be really
rude to them when I was in that mood. I'd take my anger out on
anyone.

Most people find it intimidating or downright frightening to have anger directed at them. Therefore angry outbursts can be a useful way to dominate and get our own way. It may also feel good – at least for a moment – to indulge ourselves in an angry outburst. Anger can provide us with an intoxicating sense of power. Once we have made someone afraid of us we often need to do very little to maintain that fear. The memory of our anger lingers. Rather than risk further attack others often choose to go along with our demands. However, goodwill, trust and honesty are sacrificed.

Exercise: Acknowledge the Ways You Are Hurting Others at Work

As we have seen, there are any number of ways to claim power over another in the workplace. Clearly identifying destructive behaviour is an important step. To clarify the ways you are hurting other people consider the following statements. Check (✔) those behaviours you clearly identify as ones you use, and define how true these are for you by choosing between the options. Put a question mark (?) beside those you are not so sure about.

_____ I sometimes/often talk down to someone at work in a condescending way.

_____ I use subtle tactics like black looks, harsh tone, dismissiveness or innuendoes to make someone feel uncomfortable.

_____ I use put-downs to make people at work feel inadequate.

_____ I am can be cutting, rude and/or sarcastic at work.

_____ I sometimes use the silent treatment to get at someone.

_____ I have a tendency to feel superior to other people.

_____ I sometimes take out my frustrations on others with less power than myself.

_____ I sometimes become overly sharp or critical.

_____ I sometimes/often deliberately induce guilt in the other workers.

_____ I sometimes/often devalue someone at work's skills, strengths and/or intelligence.

_____ I sometimes/often undermine someone by gossiping, backstabbing, criticising or condemning them.

_____ My manner is often controlling and/or intimidating.

_____ I sometimes/often find fault just so I have an excuse to vent my frustrations on someone at work.

_____ I sometimes/often direct angry outbursts at other people.

_____ I usually make sure other people don't witness my hurtful behaviour.

_____ I sometimes justify my behaviour by telling myself other people are at fault.

_____ I sometimes/often/always deny the seriousness of my behaviour and refuse to take responsibility for it.

This chapter has explored the various ways we can hurt others in the workplace. If you are hurting others and have honestly identified and acknowledged this you have taken a significant step towards change. It is not until we admit to the ways we are being destructive that we can do something about it.

CHAPTER 10

Counting the Cost of Power Games

The price paid for power games in terms of human suffering can be enormous: heartache, despair, shame, confusion and fear; loss of self-esteem, confidence, health, dignity, financial resources and relationships. This price is paid not only by the person on the receiving end but often by the one doing the hurting as well. When power games are a feature of relationships there are no winners – certainly the person who is undermined doesn't win, but neither does the person doing the hurting. Instead people get caught in constant struggle and pain. The way to 'win' in any type of relationship is to create a relationship founded on integrity and trust.

In this chapter women talk about the price they, and people around them, have paid for their hurtful behaviour. They all agree that having peaceful, respectful relationships is far preferable to any fleeting feeling of triumph gained at another's expense.

THE COST TO OUR RELATIONSHIPS

For most of us our relationships are of prime importance. The quality of our lives can often be gauged by the quality of our relationships.

Ideally through our relationships with others we are known, appreciated, validated and nurtured. Obviously if we are consistently hurting others our relationships will mirror this. Rather than life-enhancing closeness and care we will have conflict and tension. When we are using destructive power games with people – whether in the home, family, workplace or community – our relationships are likely to suffer in all kinds of ways.

Loss of Trust

Trust is the foundation of any healthy, respectful relationship. In close relationships trust makes it safe to reveal our real self and share our heart. Naturally we don't want to risk the most precious and vulnerable parts of ourselves being attacked and wounded. Even in relationships that are mostly functional, such as those in the workplace, giving of our best requires a degree of trust that people will treat us with kindness.

> I know my aggression has affected all my relationships. People don't trust me. Even my partner doesn't trust me. I can't say I blame him after what I've done but I've changed now. I just wish he could see that. Sometimes I get pissed off because he's still keeping his distance but I guess he has the right to keep his defences up. I've just got to hang in there and make sure I don't go back to my old ways, and hope that sooner or later he will see I've changed and really trust me again.

When trust has been destroyed by hurtful behaviour it is often a long process to rebuild it. If people feel betrayed by us or lose confidence in us because of our destructive ways we need to adopt and maintain respectful behaviour and to give them the time and space needed to develop trust in us again.

Loss of Closeness

People are often very quick to sense whether or not others are safe. If they perceive us as unsafe they may avoid us, or stay guarded and proceed with caution.

> *My bullying certainly didn't bring me any happiness. At work I could see people shying away from me – they just didn't want to know me. I think they found me quite unpredictable. Sometimes I could be nice but other times I'd be short and rude and I could be quite cutting. It certainly didn't win me any friends. In the end I felt really isolated.*

When our behaviour causes other people to distance themselves from us, there is no basis for developing genuine trusting relationships and we can be left feeling alienated and alone. Relationships may continue on a superficial level but usually there is an underlying emptiness – a sense that there is no real connection with those around us. Although at times our hurtful behaviour can be a cry for closeness and support, this cry is unlikely to be heard or responded to as we would like.

> *My nastiness created a huge gulf between us. For me I'd fire up and fly off the handle and say my piece and then it would be all over and I'd forget all about it. But Ann would withdraw and avoid me for hours, sometimes days. Over time I could see that she was distancing herself more and more from me.*

Loss of Honesty

Many people cope with being around a dominating person by attempting to please. While at one level this may feed our desire for power and superficially meet our needs, at a deeper level this usually feels unsatisfying because people are relating to us in a compliant, guarded way rather than a real way.

*I got the feeling people were humouring me all the time at work and
I didn't like it. Everyone was 'Yes ma'am, no ma'am,' and did
everything I wanted, almost before I'd opened my mouth to ask. It
used to drive me mad because it was like they were all scared of
me and they thought the best option was to bend over backwards
to keep me happy.*

When people are subjected repeatedly to overbearing behaviour
they eventually become worn down, anxious and afraid to be honest.
They often live with the sense of being under siege, ever ready for the
next power struggle.

*I knew very well Carol was terrified of me. She'd try her best to
keep me happy, try not to rock the boat and do anything to keep
the peace. She'd often clam up and only speak when she had to. I
could sense this underlying smouldering anger at me but there was
no way she'd own it. At times I'd catch such a look of loathing that
I was sure she hated me.*

Loss of Respect

Everyone has different ways of coping with power plays. Some people will
refuse to let that person affect them by ignoring or dismissing them.

*I used to have a mean temper and everyone knew it. I was always
losing my cool, especially when I'd been drinking. But what I found
after a while was that people didn't take me seriously, even when I
was quite serious and rational. It was like they didn't even listen
to me a lot of the time. They seemed to just think, 'There she goes
again,' and just switch off.*

Other people can have long memories. Even if we change our
hurtful ways it may be a long time before they begin to see us with
new eyes.

I wasted a lot of time and energy degrading other people that I could have put into helping myself. Looking back now I see my behaviour hasn't done anything to help me. It didn't do anything for my self-esteem or my reputation. I've found it takes a long time to shake off the reputation you get.

Loss of Goodwill and Co-operation

In the short term playing ongoing power games may coerce or shock the other person into submission, but people usually begin to feel resentful and fed up if they are constantly being manipulated into compliance. If a person feels incapable of standing up to us and challenging us directly then it is likely they will find other ways of resisting our domination.

I knew Geoff really resented the way I was treating him and he had his little ways of paying me back. He'd promise to pick up something from the shop then he'd say he forgot. If we were going out he'd arrive home late because he had supposedly had a last-minute customer. Sometimes he'd make little digs at me in front of our friends or families. It was like these things were a way of getting back at me that I couldn't easily pin him down for.

Loss of Self-control and Safety

If a person is attacked often enough the time may come when he or she will fight back.

John was not a violent person but he actually did hit me once because I really hurt him. I threw the vacuum cleaner at him, so he picked up a pot plant that I loved and broke it and I saw red. I picked up a pottery bowl and threw it at him and screamed blue murder and he hit me. My eldest boy rushed into the room and took the other boy downstairs and then he came back and said to

> John, 'Leave Mum alone.' Then he said to me, 'Shut up, you've got
> to shut up. You've hurt him.' Then John said, 'I'm not putting up
> with this any longer, come on,' and the three people I cared most
> about in my life walked out the door, and I thought, 'I've really
> done it now.'

If a relationship is becoming a violent battleground both parties
need to seek immediate help. There is never any excuse for violence. It
is only a matter of time until someone is seriously hurt. For strategies
on how to stay safe see Chapter 12 'Choosing to Change', and 'Take
Time Out', p. 208.

Loss of Relationships

Everyone has a breaking point. It is possible to drive even the most
caring, committed person to the point of leaving a job or a relationship, or turning their back on us.

> I used to worry myself sick wondering how much longer my
> partner would stay. I was really terrified of being left, but it
> seemed almost inevitable. I'd had several relationships break up
> because of the way I was, and it was more than I could bear to
> think of losing another one.

THE COST TO OTHERS

We may try to pretend our destructive behaviour has little or no
impact on the person we are hurting, but deep down we know it does.
The experience of being on the receiving end of power games has been
well covered in Chapter 5 'The Impact of Power Games'. Although it
may make painful reading, especially if we identify with the one who
is inflicting the pain, it is important to read this chapter to get a true
sense of what it is like to be hurt by power games. This can provide a

strong incentive to change. It can also help us to stay out of denial when we are hurting others. It becomes much more difficult to misuse our power over someone when we allow ourselves to acknowledge the way we are wounding them.

> *I had no empathy with my daughter. It was like I wasn't able to look at her and imagine how she was feeling. I did know what it felt like to be bullied, though. My father had yelled at me and abused me. If I could have taken that on board, or someone had been able to show me at the time that I was doing exactly what my father had done to me, maybe I could have done something about my bullying then.*

THE PERSONAL COST

After they have deliberately hurt others most women describe feeling bad about themselves and their lives. The more intolerable our behaviour becomes to the people around us, the more miserable our own lives often get, as the following women share.

Isolation

> *I was so lonely I didn't have any real friends. It used to really hurt seeing the others going out together after work to have fun and I'd just be going home to an empty house and an empty life.*

Decreasing Self-esteem

> *I felt like a piece of shit because of my attitude and the manipulation and the hurt that I was causing along the way. I could see it all so clearly but it was like I was stuck in this rut and I didn't know how to get out.*

Sense of Hopelessness

I felt so worthless and I thought I had nothing there at all to work with. How was I going to find anything good or nice about myself? I remember standing in front of the mirror and looking at myself. I was overweight, I was unhappy, my life was just totally unmanageable and I thought it would always be like that.

Feelings of Helplessness and Horror

I'd get to a point of absolute desperation. I'd be telling people to do something, and then I'd just lose it. Afterwards I'd feel like I was the lowest of the low. The worst thing was realising that I was doing what had been done to me and I knew what that felt like – that was the most horrifying part. I knew I was wrong and it was so destructive.

Increasing Defensiveness

I am very strong-willed and the walls just got thicker and thicker and higher and higher to the point where no-one could get through them. Inside was this angry, shut-off, 'I'll cope with it', 'I'll handle it' person.

Compounding Misery

My life was a mess. I had financial problems up to my eyeballs. I was always drinking and taking drugs. I hated the things I was doing. The way I spoke to people, the way I treated some of my friends, everything. I couldn't understand how I'd turned into such a horrible person.

Increasing Agitation

I was just filled with so much anger. I was wired. I just couldn't sit still, I was so uptight. Often my stomach would be churning and my heart racing and I'd feel like I couldn't breathe. Sometimes my head would be pounding and I'd literally feel like I was going to throw up.

Declining Health

I was forever getting sick. I think it was because of the stress I was going through with what I was doing. I was just constantly off work. I seemed to catch every virus that was going. Then my heart started to play up and I got really frightened.

Exercise: Acknowledge the Cost of Your Power Games

This chapter highlights the fact that when we use hurtful power we undermine both our own integrity and self-esteem and other people's sense of confidence and trust. Check (✔) each statement you clearly relate to and put a question mark (?) beside those that are partially true for you.

_____ I sense that people are apprehensive and afraid around me.

_____ I know people find me unpredictable and moody.

_____ I experience a lot of conflict in my relationships.

_____ People often let me have my own way to keep the peace.

_____ I've noticed some people are withdrawing or avoiding me because they feel unsafe.

_____ I've lost relationships that were important to me because of the way I behave.

_____ I sense others are losing respect for me.

_____ My mental and physical health are beginning to suffer because of my destructive behaviour.

____ People often feel the need to defend themselves against me.

____ I often hurt other people's feelings.

____ People I care about have lost trust in me.

____ I feel bad about myself because of my behaviour.

____ My important relationships are based on fear rather than respect and positive regard.

____ I sense other people's self-esteem and confidence are being undermined by my behaviour.

Facing up to the misery we are causing takes courage but it is vital. By honestly counting the cost we take another step out of denial. This brings us closer to being able to create healthy, satisfying relationships.

CHAPTER 11

What Drives Us?

When we are playing power games we usually believe at the time that there are compelling reasons to do so. Later, when we have calmed down, we may realise that we have overreacted or misread the situation and begin to feel bad. This awareness is uncomfortable so it is often pushed away. We may try to squash the nagging feelings of self-doubt and guilt by denying we did anything wrong, pretending it was only a small incident or blaming the other person for causing the problem. That way we can avoid facing the painful truth about our own behaviour.

People who acknowledge that they frequently use power games often describe feelings of helplessness, of 'not knowing what came over me'. Despite repeated resolutions that they 'will never do it again' they find themselves engaging in the same pattern of behaviour over and over with an increasingly destructive impact on themselves as well as those around them. They often feel out of control and confused – a victim of forces that are largely outside themselves, such as other people's 'selfish', 'stupid' or 'bad' behaviour.

In order to stop hurtful behaviour it is necessary to turn your focus toward yourself: to gain some understanding of the underlying issues that are prompting you to act as you do and to begin to practise more respectful ways of interacting. In this chapter women describe some of the forces they believe were driving them to overpower others. The checklist and questions at the end of the chapter will help you to clarify the particular factors that are contributing to your behaviour. Having clearly identified these issues you are in a better position to begin to address them.

Feeling Under Constant Stress

My anger comes on from a build-up of all sorts of things. I get really tired sometimes and I still have to carry on, dropping the kids off at school and picking them up, and working during the day. Then I come home and start all over again and help the kids with their homework, cook the dinner and do the washing. I'm going until 10 o'clock at night and I think, 'Why can't you do something?' Instead of saying, 'Could you please?' I just build it up and then I explode.

Women are under more pressure now than perhaps ever before, with the constant juggling of workplace and career expectations as well as the demanding homemaking and child-rearing tasks that have always been expected of us. Under this kind of relentless pressure some women begin to react badly.

Many women run themselves into the ground doing things for everyone else. Then when they are feeling exhausted and desperate for some support and none is forthcoming they become hurt and angry. From this place it is easy to start to feel used and cheated and to take this out on other people.

Trying to Meet Impossible Standards

I can see now that I used to be really abusive at work, but at the

time I didn't think of it that way. I felt under so much pressure in
the job, there was always so much to do. I had these incredibly high
standards for myself and I was driven to meet them. But the
harder I worked, the more work piled up on me. I expected my staff
to be as full on as me.

As women many of us live with the constant strain of other
people's impossible expectations. We may also hold impossible
expectations for ourselves, driving ourselves on in a relentless quest to
meet society's ideal of the perfect woman: organised, well groomed,
hard-working, considerate and generous. If we get caught in a quest
for perfection it demands a high price. Our self-esteem may be based
on our achievements rather than who we really are. We may hide our
'imperfections' (as we see them) and present instead an image, rather
than sharing our inner world of doubts, fears, thoughts, feelings and
dreams. We may feel a gnawing sense of discontentment and find it
difficult to feel satisfied with what we do achieve. No matter how hard
we strive we just can't quite measure up. Inside we judge ourselves
harshly. Often we also project our high, rigid standards onto others
and find them wanting. We may have little tolerance for their mistakes
or our own.

I admit I like everything my way. It helps me to feel in control. I
absolutely hate things becoming disorganised or something
unexpected happening, which of course happens all the time. It
completely throws me and I get really wound up and panicky. I just
can't stand it. That's when I become aggressive and give people a
hard time.

Wanting a 'Quick Fix'

Sometimes when I'm lashing out at the kids I just want them to
shut up and do as I say – now. It does get them moving when I

*really let them have it, but the more I do it the worse it all gets. I
end up feeling like an ogre and the kids end up resentful and defiant.
Really it brings everyone down.*

If we become heavy-handed enough people will usually bow to our
desires. They are afraid of what might happen if they don't. Forceful
power can bring about quick compliance and this can save time and
energy. We don't need to stop, think, plan or negotiate. Because power
games can be a 'quick fix' we can fall into a pattern of habitually using
them. Unfortunately it often requires an increasing amount of
pressure to achieve the same result.

Desperately Wanting Attention

*I felt as if Sue just couldn't be bothered with me any more. I was
just a nuisance. The more I thought like that the more desperate I
felt. I kept looking for reassurance and trying to make her come
round. I'd give her the guilts by telling her, 'I have a really lonely
life. I've got no real friends. You're the one I'm closest to. I miss
you,' but all this did was make matters worse. When she did come
round she was withdrawn and I could sense she resented my
demands.*

We all like to get what we want. At the same time we usually learn
to tolerate the frustration we feel when this doesn't happen. If our
needs have been largely unmet as a child we may continue to struggle
with intense feelings of insecurity and neediness. We may try to make
up for our childhood deprivation by constantly demanding others
meet our needs. We are hungry for attention, approval, reassurance,
affection and love. We may use whatever means we have to make the
other person do what we want, including making them feel guilty,
obligated and/or inadequate.

Talking Ourselves into Anger

*Often I overreacted and got furious with my assistant. I've come
to realise it was coming out of what was going on in my head, not
reality. She'd do something annoying like misplacing some papers
or forgetting to pass on a message and I'd be down on her like a ton
of bricks. Even though it was a totally innocent mistake, in my
mind it was like she'd done it on purpose, just to provoke me. I'd
be telling myself, 'I've told her a thousand times to be careful. She
never takes any notice of me. She's just plain sloppy.' Really we
were both under pressure and it was understandable that the odd
thing would get missed, and I'd remember that later, but at the
time I convinced myself that she was lazy and just didn't give a
damn.*

The way we interpret events and what we tell ourselves about
experiences has a profound effect on both our feelings and our
behaviour. Negative thoughts and assumptions can trigger anger.
When this anger gets converted into hurtful behaviour the problems
begin. If a person has offended us in some way we may leap to the
defensive and begin to tell ourselves a story that casts the other person
as the wrongdoer. In our mind we condemn the other person and
ascribe motives that may be completely false or at best highly
exaggerated. We feel indignant and self-righteous: the innocent
victim. We are hurting and it is the other person's fault. We feel
justified in 'hurting them back'.

Being Too Afraid to Let Go

*I was so scared my children would make the wrong decisions and
stuff up their lives. I thought I was the only one who knew the
'right' way to go. I'd had such a hard time myself, I didn't want to
see them making the same mistakes as I had. But really I took it*

*to the extreme and became quite forceful. I just didn't give them
room to grow and become independent.*

Socialised as we are to care for others, it can be a challenge to know
where the limits lie. It can be a fine line between helping and taking
over. Doing too much for others can undermine their confidence and
competence and discourage self-reliance. We may be unclear about
where our responsibility ends and when we are going too far. We may
feel compelled to organise, worry, advise, give and help. In return we
can feel entitled to expect unquestioning loyalty, compliance and
gratitude. If these are not forthcoming we may use guilt trips,
reminders about 'all I've done for you', or feel justified in striking out
punitively. Unacknowledged feelings of neediness and fear may be
underlying these overpowering tactics.

Feeling Entitled

*I used to expect my partner to do everything I wanted. It was my
way or no way. If he didn't want to do it, too bad. I wanted it my
way and that was that. Why should I compromise?*

If we lack the sensitivity or empathy to identify what those around
us are feeling or have an inflated sense of our own importance we may
feel entitled to have our needs met at others' expense. We may expect
others to hang on our every word and mindlessly obey our commands.
If they refuse we may feel perfectly justified in reacting with indignation or outrage.

Our belief that we are entitled to special treatment may well
have its roots in being over-indulged as a child. If we have been constantly given messages about how special we are and indulged
to the point where we come to consider this our right, we may now
as adults continually expect others to bow to our wishes and cater
to our whims. We experience our needs and desires as all-consuming

and all-important. Others' needs are of little or no importance.

Being 'Under the Influence'

> *When I had a few drinks I'd be a totally different person. Most of the time when I wasn't drinking I'd be quite quiet and pleasant but when I got drinking it would be a different story. Someone would say something and I'd feel this rage inside of me bubbling up and that would be it – it would be all on and there'd be no stopping me. At the time I didn't care what I said or who heard me or what they thought, but afterwards I felt really ashamed knowing that they all thought that I was a really bad person.*

Using alcohol and drugs can reduce our impulse control and our ability to make safe choices when we are feeling argumentative and aggressive. If we have a problem with hurting other people, using these substances is likely to make the situation worse. When working to change destructive behaviour it is important to address these issues as well. (See 'Seek the Support You Need' p. 199.)

A Need for Control

> *Power games filled a certain need for me. I was like the family scapegoat that everyone dumped on. I was just walked all over. I was good to be yelled at and good for sex and good for people to dump on, but that was it. I wanted to have control somewhere so I took it outside. Out there I could be powerful. The more I got demoralised at home the more I wanted to hurt somebody else, to put them in that position. It made me feel much better.*

If we feel disempowered in one aspect of our lives we can resort to taking power over people in another setting in an attempt to relieve our feelings of helplessness.

Fear of Abandonment

I was so frightened of losing Sue, I didn't want to let her out of my sight. Naturally she wanted to have her own friends but I just felt so insecure that I hated it. When she did go out I'd just sit there and worry myself sick about what she was up to. I'd imagine all sorts of possibilities and get really stewed up. Then when she came home I'd just let her have it.

If we are afraid we are going to lose someone who is important to us it can be excruciatingly painful. This is especially true if we have had issues of abandonment as a child. When we act out our feelings of desperation, jealousy and pain the outcome is likely to be destructive for ourselves as well as the other person.

I now realise that what triggered me into an episode of abuse was the terror of abandonment. When there was conflict Peter would withdraw and I'd feel betrayal and frustrated that he wouldn't talk, terror that he didn't care about me, self-disgust, a whole lot of stuff I just couldn't deal with. So I became more and more emotionally abusive and I'd scream at him and he'd shut me out more and that would trigger me even more. My underlying thought was, 'I'm not worthy of this man's love and therefore he's going to leave me because I'm a bad person.' In a way it was like a self-fulfilling prophecy.

Fear and Guilt

I could see the pain I was inflicting on people, yet I felt powerless to stop it. Strange as it might seem, knowing I was turning everyone against me just seemed to make me worse. I felt driven by my fear of losing everything that was important to me and by my own guilt. I felt so ugly inside. I felt like my life was

spiralling out of control and I couldn't seem to do anything
about it.

Our feelings of fear and guilt can provide us with useful signals that
something is wrong and alert us to the fact we need to change. When
we experience feelings of guilt after hurting someone our conscience
is letting us know we are behaving harmfully. If we fail to listen to this
signal and make changes we are likely to feel increasingly anxious. We
may be afraid others will find out about our power games, that they
will think badly of us, that our behaviour will jeopardise our job or
relationship or that we will drive others away. Often these fears are
quite valid. If we choose to ignore or override these feelings we can
become locked into increasingly destructive behaviour.

Looking For an Outlet for Tension

Sometimes my anger would just happen, like a mood swing, like a
pendulum. It was kind of like tension reduction. Like I had to
release it, to get rid of it. I had to get it out. People never knew
when it was going to happen next. Everything would be going
along absolutely fine and all of a sudden I'd be off. Sometimes I'd
know I was going to blow, but more often than not it would just
happen. So sometimes I was conscious of it and sometimes I
wasn't.

Our power games may result from intense emotions that we feel
desperate to release. If we have learned to cut off from our feelings for
whatever reason then we will be less aware of our building stress and
anger. It may then feel as though our anger just explodes and we may
believe that we have no control over our hurtful actions.

It was like a cycle really. I'd feel a build-up of tension and fear, then
John would do something, or not do something, and that would

> *trigger me into a rage. After the blow-up I'd feel sick, guilty and*
> *remorseful. I felt totally out of control and terrified that I was*
> *destroying what I needed the most. Filled with self-disgust, I used*
> *to apologise. I was on a cycle and I didn't know how to get off it.*

Lenore Walker (1979) was the first person to identify a cycle that commonly gets played out when people are hurting others.[1] It begins when the person starts to become tense. Rather than talk about what they are feeling they begin to stew: they think angry thoughts, feel agitated and focus on someone else as the source of their discomfort. They begin to act more aggressively and perhaps set the other person up for conflict by fault-finding. This is followed by the 'blow-up' stage where hurtful behaviours are used to discharge the tension and anger. Finally there is the guilt and remorse stage where the person often promises not to hurt again.

If we keep going around this cycle we are likely to feel increasingly helpless. Over time we can find ourselves going through this cycle faster and more destructively. Our tension may build more quickly, we may release this tension in increasingly aggressive ways and we may gradually give up apologising and attempting to put things right. We are also likely to feel worse and worse about ourselves.

Enjoying the Payoffs

> *Jan always did everything I wanted, especially if I got shitty. For*
> *a long time I didn't want to give that up. It felt good to be fussed*
> *over and have her running around after me all the time. If I'm*
> *honest, deep down I felt like there was this empty place inside me*
> *and I needed her to fill it up with her attention and love, but really*
> *there was never enough love to fill it.*

Power games can make people sit up and take notice and do as we say, at least in the short term. We may desperately want to have our needs met, even if it is at other people's expense. We may enjoy the feeling of being the one in charge, the one that others submit to. The adrenaline rush that usually accompanies anger can give us the energy and confidence to drive home our point and win the argument by insisting on having the last word. In that moment we can feel powerful, important and 'right' – maybe even invincible.

> *It felt good. It was a great feeling because I was getting my own way. It was the power of being the person who controls every-thing. It's the only feeling I was able to cope with, because I was safe. If I was in total control, then I didn't have to worry about being abandoned or being in any sort of jeopardy.*

Repeating Past Patterns

> *My bullying all started in my childhood. I was bullied by my parents and because of that I was very withdrawn at school and I was picked on. I got to about 13 and I decided that was it, and I completely changed roles. It was like everyone had been dumping on me, and I'd had enough. It was, 'Don't step on me because I'll step right back.' Yet at home I was still really withdrawn, never spoke unless I was spoken to, avoided everybody, did as I was told, was very, very compliant. Didn't rock the boat at all.*

If we have witnessed or experienced destructive power games as a child we are likely to carry painful memories of the people we cared about and relied on being humiliated and hurt, or behaving aggres-sively. We may carry these early wounds into adult life and as a result struggle with shaky self-esteem, doubts and fears, a sense of helpless-ness and maybe rage.

> *I had so many unresolved issues from my childhood when my mother was so abusive towards my father. After I got married I*

began to repeat the same pattern of behaviour. I'd married a man
who was a 'peace at any price' man and that fanned my fury. I just
hated Paul for being so subservient. I wanted him to fight back, but
he didn't have it in him. I felt out of control and I knew I was
screaming out for him to take control. As things got worse I felt as
if I was possessed, like I had no power, like a total victim, even
though it was me doing the abusing. I didn't have any sense of
myself at all, I didn't know who I was. I hated myself for what I
was doing but it seemed like I had no way of stopping my
destructive power. I was terrified of destroying my weak husband
by my abuse, yet I watched in helpless horror as I saw the same
scenario unfold in my marriage as I'd seen in my parents.

When we have lived through early abuse the pressure to repeat our
first model of 'relating' by hurting others may feel compelling and all-
consuming. This is especially likely if our current situation bears some
similarity to our early experience. Our childhood legacy may continue
to affect us consciously or unconsciously throughout much of our
lives unless we take the time to honestly address our hurts. If we are
repeating destructive past patterns it is vital to acknowledge this. (See
'Healing Past Hurts', p. 233.)

Parenting the Way We Were Parented

My mother knew I was taking my frustrations out on my son and
she'd say to me, 'You're too hard on that boy,' but everyone else in
the family was saying, 'No you're not. You'll get his respect,'
because they were doing the same thing to their kids. It was
normal. It was okay because that was what we had when we were
kids. That was supposedly discipline and getting our respect. I was
in turn re-enacting the same things. I'd tell myself that my boy
was going to be okay in the long term because he was going to

> *respect me. Now I know that it doesn't help at all, it just keeps the*
> *whole cycle of abuse going.*

Some people still believe that physical punishment is the only
effective way to discipline a child. In the name of discipline we may
direct our anger at our children. The line between discipline and abuse
can be crossed unwittingly, especially where there is anger involved.
It is a myth that we will gain children's respect by physically punishing
them. Those of us who have been hit severely as children could ask
ourselves if it made us respect that person or resent and fear them.
True respect is earned by positive means rather than demanded as of
right. The link between children suffering early abuse and behaving
abusively or in a disempowered way as adults themselves is all too
apparent.

> *I've been fighting to survive from a very young age and that just*
> *carried on. It was sort of like it was bred in us. That was just the*
> *way the world was: you drank, you did your best and if you needed*
> *to you fought. And whenever I felt I was going to enter into a place*
> *of fear I just came out with my aggressive side, to show people and*
> *let people know and send that vibe out to people: 'Watch what you*
> *do. If you don't you'll end up getting hurt.'*

Sometimes whole families subscribe to the belief that harshness
and physical punishment are acceptable child-rearing practices. The
challenge and hope is for individual members to rethink these dictates
and to develop gentler methods of discipline which take into account
the child's vulnerability and feelings into account. (See Chapter 14
'Parenting with Personal Power'.)

Acting Out of Unbearable Pain

> *I'd been sexually abused as a child and I coped by withdrawing into*

myself. My sister had always hated me. She hit me and blamed me
for everything and gave me a really hard time. Then one day she
just spat out at me, 'You killed Mum because you shouldn't have
been born. She wasn't meant to have any more kids.' My natural
reaction was, 'I've had enough of you,' and I just punched her. I
lost it and I saw red and I couldn't stop hitting her. The pain had
built up over the years. I'd had enough of her bullying, bitching,
everything. I'd never taken my anger out on anyone before. That
was the beginning of my violence. I'd had it with everybody. I
wouldn't stand for it any more. Once I started letting that anger
out I couldn't stop. It was the beginning of several years of
violence.

Some people experience more suffering than any human being should ever have to bear, and from this place of deep hurt they lash out to wound those around. If we often feel extreme rage or other intense emotions then this is usually not just about the immediate issue. When our feelings are overwhelmingly painful and intense and our emotions are running high we are often being triggered by something from our past. Deep wounds need attention, love and care. If you are being driven by uncontrollable rage it is important to seek the help of a professional psychotherapist or counsellor to deal with the source of the pain. For information about staying safe see 'Take Time Out', p. 208.

Exercise: Identify the Underlying Issues

As we have seen, there are many issues that may be contributing to our tendency to use destructive power. Once we are able to identify these issues clearly we can then begin to work on them to free ourselves from their grip. To clarify your own situation check (✔) each of the following statements you identify with and put a question mark (?) beside those that are partially true for you. There are no right or wrong answers. The statements are simply to help you to gain insight into what factors are important to you.

_____ I misuse my power when I'm feeling overloaded and stressed.

_____ I am a perfectionist and judge myself and/or others harshly.

_____ I often wind myself up by telling myself negative things about other people.

_____ I feel driven by feelings of guilt, anger and/or fear.

_____ I feel compelled to repeat past patterns of destructive behaviour.

_____ I can't stand losing an argument. I like to 'win'.

_____ I often behave destructively when I feel jealous.

_____ I don't know how to ask for what I want so I use guilt trips as a way of getting my needs met.

_____ When others disagree with me I find it difficult to cope with the frustration.

_____ I get so wound up when I don't get what I want that I 'lose it'.

_____ It is enormously important for me to be in control.

_____ I feel entitled to have other people do things my way.

_____ I use power games to counteract my fear of rejection and/or abandonment.

_____ I believe that using power games is the best way to resolve conflict.

_____ I get very easily hurt so I use power games to protect my vulnerability.

_____ I enjoy the feelings of power and control.

_____ I attempt to control other people because I secretly fear they will leave me.

_____ Quite minor situations often trigger intense emotional reactions in me.

_____ I often use hurtful power to teach others a lesson.

_____ It is important for me to feel needed so I seek to make the other person dependent on me.

_____ When I feel hurt I want to make the other person hurt as well.

_____ Using power games gets the tension out of my system.

_____ I often lash out when feeling impatient.

_____ I often use power games to cover my sense of powerlessness.

Questions to Consider

To reflect on your situation in more depth answer the following questions:

▶ What have you learned about yourself from reading this chapter?

▶ What particular needs are you attempting to satisfy by your use of power games:

_____ A need for control?

_____ A need to feel more powerful?

_____ A need to release tension?

_____ A need to be needed?

_____ A need for attention?

_____ A need to feel more secure?

_____ A need to be cared for?

▶ Have you identified any issues that stand out as needing special attention? Check the comments that you relate to:

_____ I need to learn how to manage my anger.

_____ I need to find ways to heal my past hurts.

_____ I need to find ways to reduce my stress.

_____ I need to improve my ability to communicate my feelings and needs.

_____ I need to develop more assertive ways to express my feelings.

____ I need to learn to let go of control and/or perfectionism.

____ I need to find ways to meet my own needs and become more
independent.

____ I need to find ways to handle my intense feelings without
acting out.

To change your hurtful behaviour it will obviously be important to find ways to address the needs that you have identified. The following chapters will explore these various issues and offer strategies for change.

Facing up to the underlying issues that are contributing to your use of destructive power can be an emotional experience. If you are feeling upset after reading this chapter this is quite understandable. Be kind to yourself: this is an important journey you are on. You might like to talk through your reactions with your support person or to spend some time alone, perhaps journal-writing.

[1]   Lenore Walker, *The Battered Woman*, Harper & Row, New York, 1979.

CHAPTER 12

Choosing to Change

It is possible to transform destructive power into personal power -- to move away from hurting to a way of being that is respectful and sensitive. This process of change involves honest self-scrutiny and a commitment to develop self-control and learn new ways of interacting with others.

When we are behaving hurtfully we are usually over focused on the other person in a negative way, blaming their supposed wrongdoings and inadequacies for the conflict. To make a change we need to give up the illusion of being the wronged party and take responsibility for the hurt we are causing others. This means shifting our focus off the other person and onto ourselves; increasing our self awareness and ability to manage our responses in less destructive ways.

It will be necessary to share power, compromise, let go of the desire to control people and situations and learn more effective ways of communicating and handling conflict.

Making a change also involves a willingness to be more gentle with yourself. When we are hard on other people we are often equally hard on ourselves. The harshness and criticism we direct at others is often a reflection of the harshness and criticism we experience within. Therefore becoming kinder, more accepting and gentle will be a two-way process of inner and outer change: learning to be more sensitive to your own needs and vulnerabilities as well as those of other people. As you find ways to be more patient, tender and loving towards yourself you can also offer this to others.

These kinds of changes may be a big challenge but the rewards are truly worthwhile. It takes courage to commit to change. As much as you may want to change, the thought of giving up power games can be threatening. You may fear that if you become more gentle other people will take advantage of you. It may be inconceivable to imagine having harmonious, mutually supportive relationships based on equality. You may feel so out of control you fear it will be impossible to stop your hurtful behaviour. This is not true! As you begin this journey trust yourself to find ways to cope with the challenges presented by this process of change. Hold on to the belief that your changes will have a positive outcome for you, as well as those around you. It *will* happen if you commit to the process.

This chapter looks at ideas and strategies for change as women share their experiences, insights and wisdom. As you work your way through this chapter you will probably be hoping that relationships will improve as a result of the changes you make. This is not unrealistic but it is important to keep your focus on your own behaviour. When there is conflict we have control only over what *we* say and do. We cannot force anyone else to change his or her behaviour.

Clarify Your Goals

Having got this far you probably have some idea of the changes you would like to make. The next step is to commit these to writing. This transforms your hopes into specific goals which can be referred back to, evaluated and ultimately achieved. The following questions will guide you in a process of taking stock of where you are now, where you want to go and what might challenge and sustain you along the way. Write the answers to these questions in your journal and refer to this often, especially if you begin to lose focus or doubt your ability to make the changes you desire.

Questions to Consider

> What behaviours do I want to change?

> What might I need to give up to achieve these goals?

> What am I hoping to gain by making these changes?

> What are my doubts and fears about change?

> What might challenge me or stop me achieving these changes?

> How will I overcome these obstacles?

> What personal attributes do I have that will help me: courage? willingness? commitment? determination? tenacity? honesty?

Write about each of these attributes in your journal, clarifying how they will help you. Add any other attributes that may also assist you in achieving your goals.

Recognise That You Have a Choice

When we act hurtfully we may believe that we have lost control and therefore are not responsible for our actions. In fact during conflict we make many choices. We can choose to:

> continue to discuss an issue even though we are becoming unreasonable;

> continue to override the other person's 'no' and push to get our own way;

> interrogate the person about what they have been doing;

> speak in a demeaning tone;

◗   put down and criticise the other person;
◗   set them up and bait them.

Each of these choices for destructive behaviour will result in a hurtful outcome. *Acknowledging that we have a choice about our destructive behaviour is a powerful step towards change because it means we can make different choices if we decide to.* For example, rather than behaving destructively you may choose to:

◗   take a break from what you are doing;
◗   leave a contentious issue until a better time;
◗   have some time alone to calm down;
◗   stop being aggressive and listen to the other person's point of view;
◗   talk to your support person;
◗   communicate more respectfully to the person concerned about what is bothering you.

The power to make things different rests with you. The strategies in this chapter will help you to gain more awareness of when you are heading towards a destructive episode. It is then up to you to consciously make different choices. Before you act, train yourself to stop and think about the big picture of the changes you want to make and why. When you find yourself acting destructively, consistently practise stepping back and asking yourself how you would feel if you were on the receiving end. With this change in focus you will gradually develop a gentler, more compassionate attitude towards others.

Practise Letting Go of Controlling Others

Our need to control others can lead us into all kinds of intrusive behaviours: judgement, criticism, pushiness, interrogation and being demanding. We can save ourselves and the people around us a lot of stress and heartache by giving up our attempts to control. Our control tactics are likely to leave us feeling frustrated and resentful, because ultimately it is not possible fully to control other people's actions. Our attempts at control are likely to damage our relationships.

If you are prone to using controlling behaviour you need to make a conscious effort to break this life-draining habit if your relationships are to truly flourish. Letting go of control is about respecting other people's right to live their own lives. The list of rights on p. 270 will provide you with a guide as to what rights we are each, as individuals, entitled to exercise. Everyone has the right, for example, to make their own decisions and enjoy a certain amount of privacy, even within a close family.

You may be well aware of some of your control tactics but there may also be ways you are overstepping the boundaries in your relationships without even recognising it. If you are in the habit of being overbearing you need to accept that 'no' means 'no' in an adult relationship.

If you are picking up signals that a person does not want to discuss a particular subject or answer your interrogating questions, try asking yourself, 'Is this really any of my business or am I being intrusive?' If you are unsure whether someone wants your unsolicited advice try asking in an open way whether they would honestly like to hear your opinion or not. If they don't, leave it there.

When you find yourself judging and criticising others for being different you need to remind yourself that they are entitled to be different. They do not need to do things your way. Diversity is the spice of life.

Every time you feel the need to take charge and become overbearing try taking a deep breath and repeating to yourself: 'It's okay to let go.' Then consciously back off. Remind yourself that it is not up to you to take over other people's problems and make their decisions for them. It is also not up to other people to meet your needs and make you happy. Each of us has the responsibility to do these things for ourselves. (See 'Developing Healthy Boundaries', p. 225.)

Giving up control is likely to bring our underlying fears into focus. We may feel insecure or dependent, or be afraid of being rejected or abandoned. We may not trust certain people enough to let them learn, make mistakes and be responsible for their own actions. We may believe that if we let go of control our lives will become chaotic. In fact the best way to gain a sense of control is to direct your energy towards *yourself* and practise taking care of your own needs. As you make changes it will be important to face your fears honestly and to deal with them directly. The following questions will help you with this process.

Questions to Consider

Think of a situation or a relationship in which you know you are inclined to exercise too much control. Write the answers to the following questions in your journal.

▶ What effect are my control tactics having in this situation?
▶ If I gave up control in this situation how might my life be different?
▶ How do I feel about the prospect of giving up control?
▶ What are my worst fears?
▶ How realistic are these fears?
▶ How can I get my needs met without using controlling behaviour?
▶ What do I need to do for myself so I don't have to use these tactics?

Seek the Support You Need

As we curb our hurtful behaviour, having the support of other people often makes all the difference.

It has been people who have really changed it for me. Getting some friends who are real friends and who are still there the next day, after I've done something wrong. They might not like what I've done but they'll still talk to me. It's been important to let people know who I really am and how I feel. That was very difficult at first, and it still is, but it gets easier.

While it may be tempting to keep hurtful incidents to ourselves this means we miss out on the listening ear, useful suggestions and practical help other people can offer. The type and the amount of support we will need will depend very much on the degree of change we are endeavouring to make and the particular issues we are facing. For some women it is enough to have one special support person to confide in who knows what changes she is working to achieve. Others may feel the need to involve several other people or seek some professional help.

Some women find joining an anger management or support group can be wonderfully helpful and uplifting. Although joining a group takes courage when we speak honestly about our lives it is a major step towards real change.

Things started to change for me when I went along to a women's course. Before that I felt like shit every day and I gradually realised that if I continued to stay at home I was going to get totally lost there. I really needed to get out in the community to feel like I was worth something. So I took the initiative to ring the local community centre. Even though I was really scared I joined a course because I thought that maybe if I heard other women talking about what I was doing and feeling then I'd be able to share the secret about my abuse and I'd feel better. It was amazing. Just sitting there listening to the other women I realised that I wasn't alone. What that course did was to challenge my compassion. I saw that

*with my family I couldn't show any compassion and I wanted to
know, 'Why can't I? What's going on? What's so hurtful inside me
that I can't be there for them? What's happened to me?' That gave
me a place to start. When I looked at the overall picture I realised I
was feeling so guilty about what I was doing I couldn't see past that
guilt to find my way to being compassionate to the people I loved.*

Sometimes working with a qualified counsellor or psychotherapist
can offer specialist input and invaluable ongoing support for the
changes we are making.

*Counselling has helped me find solutions about how I can deal with
my anger and I've learned to stop and think. I never did that before,
I just lashed out. It was cruel what I was doing to other people.
Before I never used to speak out. Counselling has been great for me.
It's made me a stronger person. It's been a great weight off my
shoulders to be able to talk to somebody. It is telling information,
it's like tell-tales, but it's okay to tell because I can't hold them any
longer. I'm 39 and I don't want to hold on to this any more.*

If we know that alcohol and drugs are a contributing factor to our
destructive behaviour and we are serious about making changes, then
we need to stop using these substances. Often alcohol and drugs are
used to dull our internal pain and it can therefore be difficult to give
them up. Gaining support through a group such as Alcoholics Anonymous (AA) or Narcotics Anonymous (NA) or obtaining counselling
through an alcohol or drug treatment centre can be invaluable.

*I had to give up the alcohol and drugs because I knew I had to start
looking at things clearly. When I picked up the drugs and alcohol
things got distorted and I couldn't see things and hear things and
understand things clearly – see them in their true light. I knew
that my upbringing wasn't healthy, that I needed to look at it.*

There was a lot of shit under the carpet, but for a long time it was easier to keep drinking than to face those other things.

Questions to Consider

▶ Do you have enough support to enable you to make the changes you desire?

▶ What type of support do you need to help you deal with the particular issues you are facing?

▶ Are you holding back from seeking support because you feel guilty or ashamed?

▶ If you don't have support what next step do you need to make to ensure you have the support you need?

Look Behind Your Anger

Having made a commitment to change, the key to achieving these changes is to increase your self-awareness. This means learning to listen to your feelings, thoughts and the signals that tell you when you are at risk of behaving hurtfully. You can then use this information to help you discover what is happening for you and make different choices.

You may be aware of feeling angry when you decide to overpower others but anger is often a secondary emotion. Underneath your anger you are likely to be feeling other more vulnerable feelings.

I've found behind the anger there's always pain, there's always sadness, and if I push the pain away then the suffering gets worse, but if I actually breathe into the pain I notice that it'll go into something like a feeling of frustration or abandonment. I will go through a series of emotional feelings that are all related to the past and then generally it will just shift, just move and then I'll look at the person with new eyes and I usually won't feel angry at them any more.

By increasing awareness of our feelings we begin to know ourselves better and to understand why we feel compelled to behave as we do. This aids the process of change. Think back to a recent time when you were angry and behaved in a way you later regretted. What emotions were you feeling in addition to anger? Circle each feeling you remember having during that incident and add your own to this list.

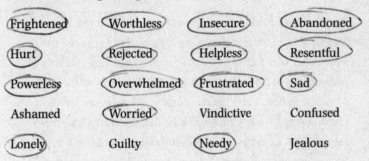

Frightened   Worthless   Insecure   Abandoned

Hurt   Rejected   Helpless   Resentful

Powerless   Overwhelmed   Frustrated   Sad

Ashamed   Worried   Vindictive   Confused

Lonely   Guilty   Needy   Jealous

Experiencing vulnerable feelings such as these can be distressing. Our anger may distract us from this discomfort and temporarily help us to feel more powerful. Anger is a handy mask we can use to prevent the other person from knowing how we really feel. However, if we habitually use anger as a defence we prevent ourselves from growing. In effect, we avoid acknowledging and working through our underlying feelings. We don't find forthright ways to deal with the real issues in our lives. Rather than taking our anger out on another person we need to spend time taking care of our hurt self. We then need to decide what action (if any) we will take to deal with the situation in a forthright but non-abusive way. (See 'Find Ways to Soothe Yourself', p. 210, and 'Speak Out Instead of Acting Out', p. 212, for suggestions on how to do this.)

If you have a tendency to numb out your vulnerable feelings or cover them over by becoming angry it will be important for your growth and self-awareness to practise gradually experiencing them. They are a rich source of information about your inner world and the values that are important to you. Consciously allowing your feelings to surface may be unfamiliar and scary, so you will need to go slowly and be very gentle with yourself. It may take time to discover the variety of feelings you have and understand what these feelings are telling you about yourself. This self-knowledge is vital to your gaining a sense of self-acceptance and personal power.

> It has been an awesome process having to live with my feelings. Some days I sit there and a feeling happens and I honestly don't know what that feeling is. I can be sitting there and suddenly I remember what I did to someone once. And I think about it and it's a horrible feeling. Memories come back – things I haven't thought about for ages. I remember things today that I didn't even remember doing at the time. It has been important to sit with the feelings and to talk through them, just to get them out of my system. I now know I have a right to be here, I'm allowed to cry if I want to cry, I do have a right to be able to express how I feel, and I do have a right to express myself on any matter.

Having understood what these feelings are telling you about yourself and your needs you are then in a better position to communicate with others. (See 'Speak Out Instead of Acting Out' p. 212.)

Become Aware of Your Stress Levels

If you are often upset when you behave destructively it is important to become familiar with the signals that will alert you to your escalating distress. When we recognise our rising stress levels we are in a position to consciously make constructive choices which will result in a more positive outcome. (See 'Recognise That You Have a Choice, p. 197.)

There is usually a whole sequence of feelings, thoughts and actions that lead up to an emotional outburst, but we often fail to notice these.

Out of touch with our feelings and stress levels we believe we 'lost it' instantaneously. This is rarely the case.

One way to raise our self-awareness is to monitor our bodily sensations. When we become upset most of us experience an increase in heart rate and body temperature, a knot in our stomach and/or a rush of adrenalin, as well as numerous other physiological changes. By getting to know our own responses we can use these signals to alert us to the fact that we need to take care of ourselves.

We can also think about our behaviour in a similar way. What kinds of actions do you resort to as you become upset? Some women withdraw or become distracted or forgetful. Others might start to pace around and become agitated. These actions can also be used as signals that alert us to our rising distress.

Exercise: Monitoring Your Stress Levels

Think of a recent time when you became upset and hurtful. Spend time completing the following checklist.

I remember the following physiological changes:

____ heart racing	✔ sick feeling in stomach
✔ adrenaline rush	____ rise in body temperature
____ sudden headache	____ stiff neck and shoulders
____ difficulty breathing	____ dizziness
✔ body tension	____ trembling hands

I remember the following changes in my behaviour:

____ I became clumsy	✔ I raised my voice
____ I became sarcastic	✔ I began to swear
✔ I slammed things around	____ I went quiet
✔ I sped up	✔ I paced around
____ I talked over people	✔ I became abrupt and snappy

Make a note of any other signals you remember. Now go through and number the signals, from the first ones you experienced to the later ones. These early signals are the ones you need to watch for in future. As soon as you notice the signs that your stress levels are rising you need to decide to do something to calm yourself down. As your distress rises your desire to act aggressively is also likely to increase. It is therefore important to take preventative action in the early stages. Don't wait until you are really wound up. See 'Find Ways to Soothe Yourself' p. 210.

Avoid Reacting Impulsively

It is often a mistake to react quickly when upset. Strong emotions such as anger, fear or vindictiveness distort our perceptions, block our thinking capacity, cloud our judgement and override our good intentions. When we are upset it may feel good and 'right' to lash out. When we calm down we realise too late the injustice and inappropriateness of our actions.

It is important to develop the habit of thinking before you act. There is a big difference between feeling upset or angry and acting destructively. We are entitled to our feelings but we have a responsibility to express them in ways that are sensitive to and respectful of other people. This requires thought! The following woman describes the way she lets her new self-awareness guide her.

> *I walk away now and think about things rather than just instantly hitting out. I don't let my anger get to the stage where I lash out. I either sit down and talk to the person or go away and think before I say something. In my mind I go through why I got angry, what I need to communicate. Then I speak up when I'm ready. If I've totally had enough I go away for the weekend instead of losing it with them all. I just need to get away to rejuvenate, rather than*

getting to the stage where I do something and regret it later. When
I come back I'm fine.

When you recognise you are getting upset, pull back from the conflict and create some physical and emotional space for yourself by leaving the room if possible. Consciously take your focus off what the other person has done to upset you. Instead, tune in to yourself and notice what is happening for you. Ask yourself the following questions:

▶ How do I feel inside?
▶ What is hurting?
▶ Is the way I am handling this situation undermining the self-respect and dignity of the other person (or myself)?
▶ What do I need to do for myself right now to take care of myself and calm myself down?

Resist the urge to return to the argument while you are wound up. Instead put your energy into calming yourself down and taking care of yourself. (See 'Find Ways to Soothe Yourself' p. 210 and 'Create a Feel Good List' p. 232 for suggestions.)

Questions to Consider

Later, when you feel calmer, take some time to clarify what is happening for you by writing the answers to the following questions in your journal. The information that can be gleaned from looking back and answering these questions provides you with insights into your actions and ideas about what you might have done differently. This is invaluable in preventing recurrences of destructive behaviour. Having completed this process you are in a better position to deal with future conflicts in a clearer and more considered way.

▶ What actions did I carry out that were overpowering (e.g. shouting, put-downs, mind games, etc.)?

- During the incident was I using anger as a defence against other, more vulnerable feelings?
- What were my underlying feelings?
- Based on my feeling(s) what was it I needed at the time?
- During the conflict what choices did I make that contributed to the hurtful outcome?
- Why did I make these choices? What was I trying to achieve at the time (e.g. to get my own way, to make the other person feel bad, etc.)?
- What was the impact on myself and the other person/people concerned?
- What other choices could I have made that would have ensured my behaviour was less destructive?
- What is the real issue here?
- Is there a deeper issue below the surface that I find hard to face?
- What (if anything) do I need to do to deal with the issue?
- What (if anything) do I need to communicate about my underlying feelings?

As with all of these exercises it is important to go gently with yourself. Heaping recriminations on yourself will make you feel worse about yourself and this is likely to exacerbate the situation. When you have explored your answers to these questions you may like to share your discoveries with your support person.

Take Time Out

A useful strategy when you are afraid that you are going to act destructively is to take time out. Time out involves putting a stop to hurtful behaviour by physically leaving for a period of time (usually an hour). Time out works best if it has been previously discussed with the other person. Let him or her know you intend to use this strategy when you think you may be at risk of becoming hurtful. Sometimes the other person may try to prevent you taking time out but don't let this deter you. Your highest priority needs to be staying safe. If you know you are at risk of acting destructively it is ultimately your responsibility to take the time you need. You can also take time out if someone is behaving hurtfully towards you.

If it is not appropriate for you to tell the other person you are taking time out and you don't want to make it obvious, for example in the workplace, you can still use this strategy. Although it may not be possible to leave the premises it is usually possible to go to the bathroom or get away from the other person (even if not for a full hour) and to focus on calming down.

Guidelines for Taking Time Out

- **Tell the person when you need to take time out.** Try saying, 'I am beginning to feel wound up. I need to take time out. I will be back in . . .'
- **Leave for the specified time.**
- **Use that time to calm down.** See p. 210 for a list of strategies for self-soothing and p. 211 for calming self-talk you can use.
- **Consider phoning your support person.** Have her or him remind you of your goal to change and help you decide what you need to do to calm yourself down.
- **Avoid alcohol and drugs, driving or putting yourself in any risky situations** such as walking alone at night.
- **Return from your time out at the specified time.**
- **Decide whether the original issue was worth discussing**. If you are feeling calm it may be appropriate to talk about the issue provided the other person agrees. If not, negotiate a later

time. (See 'Guidelines for Tackling Challenging Issues', p. 213.)

> **Repeat the time-out process** if you begin to feel wound up
> again and/or are unable to calmly discuss the issue.

Find Ways to Soothe Yourself

When we are churned up and wanting action, one of the biggest challenges we face is to calm down without resorting to hurtful behaviour
as a way of 'letting off steam'. In the heat of the moment it can be difficult to think straight so it is important to work out ahead of time what
you can do. Some possibilities include:

> Do something physical: walking, running, swimming,
> dancing, aerobics or housework.
> Do some slow, deep breathing and consciously relax on each
> outward breath.
> Phone your support person or a friend.
> Go out in the garden and pull weeds.
> Take a bath or shower.
> Play a relaxation tape.
> Take a break with a hot drink.
> Slowly stroke one arm with the opposite hand.
> Speak lovingly to yourself.
> Imagine yourself in a relaxing, safe place.
> Listen to soothing music.
> Pray.
> Cuddle your cat or dog.
> Read an inspirational book.
> Consciously stop thinking about the issue for a set period.
> Write in your journal. (Be sure to keep your focus on *your*
> feelings and actions, not on blaming and berating the other
> person.)

Exercise: Create Your Own List of Strategies for Self-soothing

Write a list of things you can do to help you calm down. Be specific. State what you will do, where you will go and who you will phone. Be sure to include some workplace strategies if there is any likelihood of your needing to implement the plan there. When you are feeling upset or at risk of using hurtful behaviour work through your list.

Use Calming Self-talk

The way we talk to ourselves internally has a profound effect on our mood. Develop the habit of noticing the negative messages you are using to justify your hurtful behaviour. Consciously put a stop to these as much as possible. Rather than winding ourselves up by telling ourselves about the other person's perceived wrongdoings we can consciously soothe ourselves by using calming self-talk. When you are upset speak to yourself gently and lovingly as you would a distressed child. This deceptively simple technique has a powerful effect. *As you give yourself the attention and reassurance you need your inner turmoil will begin to diminish.*

Possible calming messages are:
- 'It's okay, I can handle this.'
- 'This is not worth getting upset about.'
- 'I don't need to take this personally.'
- 'I can control myself.'
- 'I don't need to let this get to me.'
- 'I don't want to hurt this person so I need to calm down.'
- 'I'm choosing to act in a respectful way.'
- 'I'm feeling hurt (or frightened, upset, etc) but I can handle it.'
- 'I'm not going to take my feelings out on this person.'

Exercise: Create Your Own Calming Messages

Think of a recent time when you became upset and hurtful. Make a list of the negative messages you were giving yourself at the time. How did these messages make you feel? Did you use negative self-talk to justify your actions?

Next write a list of calming messages that you could use in a similar situation. Think about what your particular hurts and needs in the situation were and design your messages to reassure yourself. Destroy the first list. Keep your soothing messages close at hand and memorise two or three statements that are the most meaningful for you. Say these to yourself often when you are feeling distressed.

Speak Out Instead of Acting Out

It is the unspoken issues that block relationships and cause underground resentment to build and blow-ups to occur. We often act out our unexpressed feelings indirectly in our petty paybacks, sarcastic digs or sudden temper tantrums over small issues. One of the best ways to defuse pent-up feelings is to express them verbally. Even the simple act of saying 'I feel angry' will often have the effect of releasing some of the tension we are feeling, as the following woman's experience clearly demonstrates.

> *I do speak up now. Before I never used to. I just used to let it all build up and then I'd lose it. I've found many ways to deal with my hurt. Saying, 'It's not good enough, I don't want to hear that, that hurt.' Giving myself permission to be able to say those things has made a huge difference. Talking it out. Like when Simon says something to me that's quite hurtful I say to him, 'You hurt me. I really need you to know that.'*

Respectful communication is a skill that takes practice and ongoing focus and commitment. The first step is to become clear on what is really happening for you and to work out what you honestly need to say. See 'Become More Assertive', p. 129, for suggestions of ways you can communicate more effectively. In our everyday life a useful goal to is to practise communicating honestly, 'cleanly' and respectfully. By learning to listen to our feelings and ask ourselves straight questions we can effectively monitor progress.

> *Nowadays I judge my interactions with others on whether I feel sincerely good afterwards. Not feeling good because I've scored a point, but good because I've stood up for my rights in a fair way. One of the things I do after an encounter is to ask myself, 'Do I feel okay about me? Do I have any sense of guilt about what I've done to other people in that?' If I feel okay at the end of an exchange then I have a sense of pride and self-esteem. If I know what's happening, I've stated what I need to state, and I've been respectful of the other person's feelings and still set my limits, then I feel okay about what has happened. If I move to a level where I'm screaming at the person abusively, then I don't feel good about myself. That's my gauge on how I behave with other people.*

In the midst of making changes it can sometimes be difficult to know how to approach challenging issues in a new, more co-operative way. The following guidelines will help.

Guidelines for Tackling Challenging Issues

▶ **Set the scene.** Put aside a specific time for a discussion with the person concerned when you won't be interrupted. Decide together how long you will discuss the issue for. Mutually agree at the outset not to use mind games, bring up past history or denigrate or intimidate each other in any way. Commit to staying focused on the challenging issue with a view to understanding each other's position better and finding a way to resolve it for you both.

▶ **Agree to take turns to speak.** Allow five minutes each to say how you see the situation and how you feel. When in the listener role put aside your own 'story' and listen with an open mind. Be willing to let go of controlling the other person and the outcome. Accept that he or she will probably see things differently from you. Prepare yourself to hear things that you may find challenging (but don't allow yourself to be abused). Try to really understand the other person's feelings and position and speak only to ask a clarifying question.

▶ **When it is your turn to speak communicate in an assertive way.** This preserves your own dignity and that of the other person. Be willing to risk sharing your feelings. (See 'Become More Assertive', p. 129.) Beware of using harsh criticism and blame.

▶ **Work together to find a mutually agreeable compromise.** If this is not possible, agree to disagree with respect. The most important thing is that you both feel heard. Sometimes that is enough to bring about a change; sometimes it will be necessary to revisit the issue several times in this way as you work towards a resolution.

▶ **Throughout the process stay aware of your internal responses.** Use your feelings, self-talk and other signals as a guide to your stress levels. If you think you are going to behave destructively at any stage take time out. (See 'Take Time Out', p. 208.)

Prepare for Change in Your Relationships

As we change our relationships change, simply because we are no longer relating in the same way. Usually existing relationships are enhanced but the change we make may challenge some people in ways

they are not comfortable with. Some people may prefer we remained
the same even if that meant we continued to hurt ourselves and
others.

> *I've lost friends as I've changed because they couldn't accept the
> way I am now. That was really hard for me. I didn't want to let
> anyone go and I really did fight for a long time to try and get them
> to know me for who I was today and accept me as I was, but for
> some people it just didn't work. It was just too threatening for
> them. A lot of my friends have trouble handling the fact that I've
> changed. I've always been known to be big, aggressive, 'take no shit
> from anyone'. I'm just not like that any more. When I did start
> speaking my truth about how it was for me and they saw me sit
> there and cry they didn't handle it very well.*

It is sad when we have to choose between our healthier ways of
coping and having certain people in our life. However, as we continue
to heal and grow we are likely to attract new supportive people into
our lives; people who welcome us expressing our real feelings and
vulnerabilities.

If we have damaged our relationships through power games they
are not going to be repaired overnight. As much as we may long for
closer connections with those we have hurt we need to remember to
be patient. People will be understandably cautious about our new
behaviour. There is often a long period of making and maintaining the
changes before those around us feel safe enough to trust us again.

There may be a turbulent time while new behaviours are tested and
new relationship skills and patterns are developed. The person you
have been hurting may begin to express his or her previously sup-
pressed anger. If this happens try not to be too disheartened. It may
well mean that you have succeeded in creating enough emotional
safety in the relationship to allow that person to honestly express his
or her feelings. Although this can be challenging to hear, try to really

listen. This is part of the healing process. As you continue to listen, communicate constructively and maintain respectful behaviour this time should eventually pass. (See 'Talking through Past Hurts', p. 217.)

While it is important to give the other person the opportunity to express their feelings about our past behaviour this does not mean we have to tolerate shouting, put-downs or attacks on our character. If this is happening take time out and remove yourself until the situation has calmed down. (See 'Take Time Out', p. 208, and 'Guidelines for Tackling Challenging Issues', p. 213.)

If you are involved in a situation where both sides have been using power games you will be concerned not only with controlling your destructive impulses but also with protecting yourself from the other person's onslaught. Sometimes the lines between self-defence, retaliation and open aggression become blurred. You may become confused about your part in the conflict. This makes it more difficult to take positive action. If you feel unsure about where the balance of power lies, refer back to the questions in 'When Power Games Are Two-sided', p. 35, to help you clarify the dynamics in the relationship.

As you give up using destructive power in a relationship where there have been mutual power games one of two outcomes is likely. Our gentler, more respectful behaviour may prompt the other person to also make positive changes. Alternatively, the other person may continue to behave hurtfully, perhaps even escalating his or her power tactics. If this happens we need to be willing to take action. *Stopping our power games is not about becoming powerless. It is about using personal power to stand up for our rights and protect ourselves when necessary.* Chapter 7 'Becoming More Powerful' contains many strategies to help you express your power with integrity.

Talking through Past Hurts

As we achieve the changes we set out to make, and grow in self-control and self-esteem, we may become strong enough to openly discuss the previous hurtful episodes. It takes courage to face up to the hurt we have caused. A discussion may happen in an impromptu way or we may choose to initiate a time to talk about unresolved issues in an attempt to repair the damage done to the relationship. This can provide you with an opportunity to take responsibility for your destructive behaviour, and gives the other person the opportunity to say how it was for them.

> *As I've changed there has been a lot of dialogue with my children. I've had to face up to the pain and the grief and the loss that I've caused them. I've made a point of sitting down with them and telling them that I'm sorry; that I was a rotten mother and this is why. Telling them about my own childhood abuse. I've told them, 'This is our family history. This is where it has all come from, and it's got to stop here.' Of course to heal I've had to hear the pain that I've put my kids through as well. That's been really hard. Sitting and hearing that there were times that I'd really hurt them. They needed to tell me and so I listened while they laid it all out, even though it hurt like hell.*

This kind of sharing and clearing is best done in a considered way when (and if ever) you feel ready to hear things that might be painful or challenging to hear. Sometimes having a third person present is helpful. During the sharing stay in tune with yourself and notice your emotional responses. If at any time you feel tempted to revert to controlling behaviour, or if the other person is becoming disrespectful, call a halt to the process for the time being. (Also see 'Guidelines for Tackling Challenging Issues', p. 213.)

Maintaining the Changes

Having achieved our changes we need to work at maintaining them. This requires ongoing self-awareness and self-care. As disappointing as it is, it is to be expected we will have occasional times when we slip back into our old behaviours. If this happens, don't allow yourself to be too discouraged. You need to regain your focus and go back to all the strategies that have got you this far.

> *I find I have to remain very aware of my tendency to hurt people. If something upsetting is going on in my life I could still quite easily pick a fight. I haven't done it for a while but I could do it. I really have to think sometimes, 'Tonight is not a good night to go into town and have a few drinks because I'll get into trouble.' That has to be a conscious decision. I'm quite good at doing that now. I've learned that if I'm feeling at all vulnerable about anything then I can't afford to drink and I can't afford to go out. It would be easy for me to start bullying again. If I start thinking about what I can get other people to do to suit me I really have to pull myself up and say, 'Hang on,' and let people make their own decisions.*

This chapter has offered many suggestions to help you transform your hurtful power into personal power. If you find you are unable to curb your destructive behaviour by applying these strategies you need to seek professional help. A professional who is skilled in working with issues of power and hurtful behaviour can work directly with you on difficulties as they arise, supporting you in discovering the underlying issues, releasing emotions, gaining insight and working on specific strategies.

The final words in this chapter go to a woman who has not only successfully changed her behaviour but has also used her experiences to uplift other women. This is true personal power.

The transformation has been amazing for me. I never used to be able to sleep at night because of the damage I'd done, whereas these nights I can go to bed with some self-esteem. I now use my own experience to work with other women. It's amazing sitting in counselling with women who have come from their own abusive backgrounds and knowing that I can make a difference. It's okay for me to offer them something, or just myself. Having that authenticity about myself and just being there makes me feel like it has all been worth it. Empowering women to lift their heads up and walk towards the light. They are worth something. They have something to be proud of. Maybe they don't feel it at the moment but it will come.

PART FOUR

THE JOURNEY TO PERSONAL POWER

CHAPTER 13

Claiming Personal Power

The concept of personal power is as simple as it is profound. It is about expressing who we truly are by standing up for what we believe. As such it is a life-long journey towards increasing wholeness, authenticity and confidence. There are many important aspects that interweave to form the basis of personal power.

Personal power is:
- Knowing and accepting ourselves.
- Developing healthy boundaries.
- Speaking our truth.
- Taking care of ourselves.
- Healing past hurts.
- Creating strong connections.
- Living our passion.

On a day-to-day level personal power is about listening to our feelings, speaking out when we have something to say, being who we really are without apology, allowing ourselves to make mistakes, stating our limits and standing our ground. Most of us get dozens of opportunities to practise these things every day, at least in small ways.

Increasing personal power involves courage and risk-taking. *We need to learn to listen carefully to our inner self, clarify what is truly important and honour this by taking action.* The rewards are increased inner peace, healthier and more sustaining relationships and a greater ability to be a positive influence on those around us. The women who speak in this chapter share some of the ways they have discovered to heal, nourish and honour themselves as they grow in personal power.

Knowing and Accepting Ourselves

Personal power develops from self-knowledge, self-acceptance and self-love. If we are to gain true personal power it is vital we take time to know honestly who we are. We need to learn to be ever gentler and more compassionate towards ourselves: to understand where we have come from and how this influences us today, to appreciate the efforts we have made to get to this point, and to forgive ourselves for those times when we have fallen short of our own expectations.

> *My big thing was learning to tell myself that I do deserve the very best life has to offer me, and coming to really believe it. I look in the mirror now and tell myself that I love myself. When I first started doing that the tears would be running down my face and I had to look away because I didn't believe it. I used to think, 'How can you feel like that about yourself? You're nobody.' But I can do it now. I kept telling myself until I believed it. It's amazing how much difference it makes to the way I feel. I think you can turn even the bad things that happen to you into something of benefit if you try. I've found my strength from within.*

Discovering that we are not the only one coping with a particular problem can be empowering. As we share our personal stories we can draw strength and inspiration from one another. Putting our own individual story in context by seeing how it relates to other women's stories can be helpful because although we often don't realise it at the time, many of the struggles we have are shared by other women.

Questions to Consider

▶ How well do you know and accept your own story: the sorrows and joys, challenges and triumphs and the things that have influenced you?

▶ Do you have a clear sense of who you are: your strengths and vulnerabilities, the wounded parts of you, your feelings, values, opinions, hopes and dreams?

▶ Have you ever told anyone your story?

▶ If you haven't told your story what has stopped you?

▶ Have you forgiven yourself for any past 'mistakes'? If not, are you willing to?

▶ Are you able to view yourself with compassion and gentleness; at least most of the time?

Developing Healthy Boundaries

Our boundaries are the lines and limits we set to define who we are, what we want and how we expect to be treated. Our boundaries encompass 'the self' – our feelings, thoughts, values – all that belongs uniquely to the individual that each of us calls 'me'. Some of us emerged from challenging childhoods with a shaky sense of self and poorly defined personal boundaries. Our boundaries are weak, broken or non-existent. We may often be uncertain about who we are as a person or what we believe in, want or need. We don't feel entitled to set clear boundaries or expect to have our boundaries respected by others. (See 'The Impact of Our Personal History', p. 107.)

Developing healthy boundaries is a skill we can learn. It is a two-way process of setting clear limits for ourselves and being respectful of other people's limits. Our boundaries need to be flexible enough to let those we choose come close, yet strong enough to keep unwanted people at bay. We need to be able to change our boundaries depending on the situation we find ourselves in, and reinforce them by communicating assertively.

If we listen to our feelings they will give us valuable guidance about when we need to set a boundary:

- Our feeling of helplessness may be telling us someone is controlling us.
- Our trapped, frustrated feelings can tell us we are being manipulated.
- Our feelings of resentment and being overwhelmed can inform us of the need to say no to others requests and demands.

Setting boundaries involves two steps. First we need to clarify what we truly want in a given situation by asking:

- How close do I want to let this person come?
- What do I want to give and share?
- What do I choose to keep private?

Second, we need to act on our decision by stating our boundary; be honest and up front about what we are willing to do and allow and what we choose not to do. We need to practise saying no to people who would take advantage of us, take over our life or would have us take over theirs. It is empowering when we remain true to ourselves by not allowing ourselves to be bulldozed, manipulated or guilt-tripped into submission. If we have lost, or never had, a sense of power with a particular person, putting boundaries in place will be a challenging process that will take time. It is often best achieved in many little steps.

Setting boundaries with my family has been a huge task. It's been like taking my life back for myself. Before, every time something happened they'd be in there wanting to take over and tell me what I'm doing wrong and how I should be handling things. Then they'd get angry if I wouldn't take their advice. I've had to really be strong to tell them over and over, 'I don't want your advice. I'm doing things my way,' and stick to my guns. It's getting easier now though because I feel like I'm coming from a stronger place. I know I have the right to live my own life now.

We may fear that if we stand up for ourselves in these ways and tell the truth we will lose people out of our lives. It is quite true that other people may resist and resent the changes we make when we begin to set clearer boundaries, but if these relationships are based on our slavishly saying yes when we really want to say no we need to think about the personal cost of these life-draining relationships. Realistically, how long can we sustain unequal relationships that require constant giving and compliance?

Setting boundaries that define our rights and needs will inevitably bring about a change in our relationships. Some people will quickly learn that we mean what we say and may gain respect. Our increased honesty and clarity may also challenge some people to become more truthful themselves. Some relationships may deepen as a result. Other people may persist in their efforts to have us do it their way. If we stand our ground they may gradually learn that we do mean what we say and reluctantly back off. Others may be so outraged they decide to give up on the relationship and find themselves someone else to push around. This at least helps us to clarify the fact that they weren't willing to grow or change to become more respectful of our rights.

We may ourselves have a tendency to be unclear about or disrespectful of other people's boundaries. We may demand to have our own way and push others to meet our needs at the expense of their own. If we know we have a tendency to override, brow-beat, push or bully, the concept of personal boundaries can be very helpful. The bottom line is that other people have the right to make their own decisions and live their own lives. It is up to us to respect those boundaries. See 'Know Your Rights' p. 270 to gain some clarity.

Questions to Consider

▶ Do you have a clear sense of division between your problems and responsibilities and other people's, or do the lines often get blurred?

▶ Are you usually able to assert yourself when you want to?

▶ Do you do too much for other people rather than letting them take responsibility for their own life and difficulties?

▶ Do you respect other people's choices or do you push on, hoping to override them?

Speaking Our Truth

Learning to communicate assertively is an important skill in becoming more powerful. Developing assertive communication and behaviour is about finding a middle ground between passivity and aggression and claiming our own rights while respecting other people's. It is the language of equality. It lets others know that we are worthwhile persons and we also consider them worthwhile. We expect to be treated with respect and will treat others the same way. (See 'Become More Assertive', p. 129.)

In gaining personal power it's been important to learn to speak out. I used to be so scared. I was a real mouse. Often I'd be feeling upset or frustrated but I wouldn't have my say. I was frightened that if I spoke up people would resent me and try to bring me down. In fact as I've become more vocal I've found people seem to respect me more. And often they seem to be genuinely interested in what I

have to say. Finding my voice has made an incredible difference to
how I feel about myself. I used to feel invisible and helpless, like I
didn't have anything worth saying, but as I started to speak out
more I got clearer about what I felt and thought. Now I see that I
do have the right to be heard and stand up for what I believe and
that feels really great.

If we have grown up in a family where it wasn't safe to tell the truth it may be second nature to be somewhat dishonest or secretive. Honestly speaking out can feel very risky if we automatically expect a negative reaction. Socialised to be accommodating and 'nice', many of us are scarcely aware of our tendency to compromise our truth in order to please others. We pretend, hint, defer, make excuses and often hide our resentment behind a smile. We may go to great lengths to avoid doing something we do not want to do by being evasive, rather than simply saying, 'I really don't want to.' The little white lies we tell may seem a harmless, easy way out but if used habitually as a substitute for assertive communication they prevent our growth and diminish our sense of personal power.

In promoting speaking the truth we are not suggesting we should reveal our innermost selves indiscriminately to those who would hurt us or use our vulnerabilities against us. We are all entitled to keep our own counsel and to have thoughts, feelings and secrets we choose not to share. What we are suggesting is that when issues arise we practise telling the truth with the person concerned as often and as honestly as we are able. *Each time we say how it is for us we are honouring who we really are.*

When important issues are not discussed they remain lurking in the shadows of a relationship. Underlying feelings of hurt and resentment usually block the goodwill in the relationship. If not expressed openly they may be acted out destructively instead. Even though it can be a challenge at times, open communication usually restores the closeness. Speaking out honestly about what we believe does not mean we need to be harshly critical or aggressively attacking. It is important to speak our truth with gentleness and integrity. Although sometimes the truth hurts, it is not about hurting others, it is about communicating in a respectful way.

> *I'm acquiring personal power but I'm not completely there yet. I find that one of the biggest learning curves for me was to be assertive with dominant males and say, 'I don't like that, I don't agree with that.' I now say how I feel with 'I' statements, instead of dumping or going all quiet and bottling up my feelings. That's a big difference for me. Before I would have kept quiet rather than create a scene.*

Questions to Consider

▶ How honest am I in my dealings with other people?

▶ How well do people know me (what I truly think and feel)?

▶ Who do I share my most vulnerable self with?

▶ When I have an opinion that differs from other people's do I tend to:

____ resort to making hints or acting evasively?

____ stay silent to avoid conflict?

____ speak my truth?

▶ Am I happy with my level of honesty or would I like to make changes?

Taking Care of Ourselves

Self-care is about valuing ourselves enough to take our needs seriously. When we care for ourselves we make our well-being a priority. We listen to the emotional and physical signals that tell us when we are becoming overloaded and tired and take action to protect ourselves from this. *Self-care is vital to personal power.*

> *Becoming more powerful is a whole series of things; learning to listen to my instincts and feelings when I'm really stressed out and I'm feeling really bad; stopping and saying, 'Okay, I'm feeling stressed out, what can I do?' I'm getting a lot better at monitoring myself. I know now that it's okay to say, 'Stop, I need a break. I'm going to go and lie down for a while and have a rest.' It's learning to know my own limits. I don't have to be perfect. It's learning to be my best friend and if I need help ask, and if I don't get it ask someone else. Being able to accept myself where I am has been important. I don't have to explain myself to people.*

Exercise: How Good at Self-care Are You?

We all need relaxation and recreation, fun, solitude, closeness, appreciation from others and satisfying activities that give our lives meaning. Your needs are important. The more aware you are of your needs the more chance you have of meeting them. To assess your self-care habits complete the following list by checking (✔) each statement you agree with. Put a question mark (?) beside those that are sometimes true for you.

- ___?___ I listen to the emotional and physical signals that tell me I need to rest and take time out accordingly.
- ___?___ I usually speak gently and encouragingly to myself when I'm stressed.
- ___✓___ I make sure I eat nourishing food.
- ___✓___ I get adequate rest and exercise.
- ___?___ I notice my efforts and achievements and affirm myself for them.
- ___?___ I usually remember to listen to my feelings and use this as the basis for action.

_____ I tell other people when I'm under pressure and ask for the help I need.

_____ I usually pace myself to my energy levels and stop and rest when I am tired.

_____ I am able to express my ideas, opinions and feelings and make my own decisions.

_____ I usually allow myself time for rest, recreation, creative activities, solitude, fun and good company.

_____ I recognise my human limitations and am realistic about how much I expect from myself.

_____ I take time to do the things I love that feed my soul, such as connecting with nature, reading inspirational books, etc.

Questions to Consider

- In what ways are you practising good self-care?
- In what areas is there room for improvement?
- Are there changes you would like to make?
- What will be your first step towards improving your self-care?
- When will you start?

Exercise: Create a 'Feel Good' List

Rather than overloading yourself, learn to listen to your energy levels and your feelings. If you are tired and stressed you need to honour this by putting your needs first. Spend time deciding on things you can do to give yourself a boost. Here is a list of 12 ideas for starters:

- Phone a friend.
- Go for a walk somewhere peaceful.
- Light a candle and have a quiet time alone.
- Dance to your favourite music.
- Cook your favourite meal.
- Read a good book.

- ❯ Watch a funny video.
- ❯ Take yourself out for dinner.
- ❯ Have a warm scented bubble bath.
- ❯ Go to the movies.
- ❯ Go for a massage or give yourself one.
- ❯ Plan a get-together with friends.

Now write your own list. Include in your list the activities that give you a lift and those that you are good at, including anything you used to enjoy but have stopped doing. Make a point of doing some things from your 'Feel Good' list every day. Keep adding to your list as you discover new ideas.

Healing Past Hurts

If left unhealed, past wounds can continue to overshadow current enjoyment of life. We may feel stuck in the unfinished business of the past. Because we are easily hurt we may keep our emotional distance from others. Instead of living and thriving, we may expend our energy coping and surviving as best we can. These things will block our sense of personal power.

Unfortunately the way out of pain is usually through it. *Pain needs to be understood and processed if we are to move on.* If we are willing to work through the issues that are troubling us and spend time with ourselves, to cry the tears and feel the feelings associated with our hurts, we will eventually come to a place of inner peace and wholeness. When we commit to this course, the right people, books and circumstances often come into our lives to support us. Although the healing journey is different for everyone there are certain tasks that are likely to be part of the process:

- ❯ telling our story honestly to someone trustworthy;
- ❯ recognising the ways we have been wounded;

- being honest about the impact these hurts have had on our thinking, feelings and behaviour;
- expressing our grief and anger about what has happened;
- recognising and honouring the things we did to survive while deciding whether these things are still serving us;
- identifying the distorted perceptions about ourselves and our relationships that we have come to accept as true;
- changing the behaviours that are having an adverse effect on our lives and trying not to repeat past destructive patterns;
- learning to develop our capacity to tolerate and manage intense feelings;
- developing relationships that are nourishing and life-enhancing and learning to expect and accept support from other people;
- learning to express our emotional reality effectively.

Throughout our healing it is vital to take good care of ourselves. This means allowing ourselves to go at a pace that best suits us and practising being gentle and accepting of ourselves as we are right now. *We need to have compassion for our own wounding.*

Different women will find different ways to heal, as the following six women's stories illustrate.

My books have been an incredibly important part of my healing because they give me access to other people's wisdom and knowledge. They inspire me and comfort me when I'm down. It's like I've got something solid to hold on to when I start to wobble. Through books I've been able to make sense of my life and the things that have happened to me. I've been able to understand that I'm not the only one who feels like I do. I know I can heal and I can understand that it takes time, and that's okay.

I've found healing through art. I set out on a journey and I didn't know where I was going, but looking back I needed to do it. For anyone who's hurt I think it is one of the most wonderfully positive things you can do. You can express yourself through art and say what you want. I never knew that art was that deep. Things happen from right down deep within you, and you don't know they are happening. When I do the artwork I get in touch with a lot of my feelings. Finding the artist within myself has been like an incredible miracle. Whether my work is ugly or beautiful it doesn't matter. For me finding myself in that artwork is so healing. I don't think anything else could have healed me that much.

Validation has been the most important thing in my healing. Because everyone else believed enough in me and in my recovery to support me through all this, it made me realise that I was worthy of belief and support and love from people. It took those external influences to make me realise that I was worthwhile.

Fear is a really crippling emotion to personal power and I'm fighting fear by doing abseiling, where I just have to just lean back and trust the rope. That's really empowered me and given me such confidence. I'm also fighting my fear of doing things in front of other people. Those are my two big areas of empowerment.

I think my power has evolved by the work I've done on myself, the books that I've read, tools that I've received on courses. It has accumulated and eventually the gears are beginning to shift. It's a slow change but I can see that dealing with my issues, owning my stuff and working hard on myself is beginning to pay off.

It's really changed my life going to counselling. I never used to cry

– no-one used to see me cry. I used to hold it down because I would think I was so tough. But I allow myself to cry now and that's helped heaps. I come away with a feeling that someone's actually listened, someone's actually been there for me. It's kind of like a cleansing. It's saying, 'This is what happened to me' in detail and describing as much as I know and it being okay. My family are not going to get me.

While we can do a certain amount of our healing alone, we will gain from developing supportive relationships with others we can trust and safely share ourselves with. If we are deeply wounded there is no substitute for the skilled help of a well-trained professional. Psychotherapy or counselling can provide us with guidance and support. Through this safe relationship we can feel secure enough to do the work that may be too difficult to do alone. You need to seek professional assistance if you are:

▶ abusing alcohol, drugs or food in an attempt to numb out emotional pain;

▶ currently being physically, sexually or severely emotionally abused;

▶ feeling depressed and/or thinking about suicide;

▶ suffering from overwhelming feelings anger or rage that are at times uncontrollable;

▶ at risk of seriously hurting someone;

▶ feeling 'stuck' and unable to make the changes in your life you want to make despite your efforts.

Throughout the healing journey it is important to remind ourselves constantly that we *can* heal our past hurts. The human spirit is incredibly resilient. From our wounding comes sensitivity and compassion. The words of Kahlil Gibran beautifully reflect the possibility of gaining depth and wisdom through our suffering: *'The deeper that sorrow carves into your being, the more joy you can contain.*[1]

Creating Strong Connections

Having strong connections with others sustains us and enriches us on our journey and gives our life meaning. *When we link up with like-minded people we strengthen our sense of personal power.* None of us can make it on our own, and even if we could it would be a very lonely journey. We all need comfort and support, shared laughter, kind words, caring, familiar faces and honest feedback and input.

> *Friends have been my saving grace. I was very good at saying, 'I can do this, I don't need any help,' until eventually I realised that sometimes I couldn't. Sometimes people have wonderful things to offer.*

Collectively we have the power to effect amazing changes that it would be impossible to tackle alone. Women have a long history of working co-operatively. It is easy to forget that because of the collective energy of many women, women in the western world at least today have the increased freedom, rights and status that we can sometimes take for granted. Yet there is still a long way to go before we achieve true equality. Women's support of one another continues to be vital.

We have much to offer each other as women. A wonderful way to gain support is to seek a mentor. A mentor is someone more experienced than ourselves who agrees to share their knowledge, skills and experience with us. We can also offer to share our enthusiasm, encouragement and expertise with other women in this way. Alternatively we can choose to form an alliance with someone of similar experience with the express intention of supporting each other in our goals.

[1]   Kahlil Gibran, *The Prophet*, Heinemann, London, 1955.

Questions to Consider

▶ Are your connections with others as strong, close and rich as you would like them to be?

▶ If not, what needs to happen to strengthen these connections?

▶ Do you have people in your life who share similar values and are passionate about similar issues to you?

▶ Do you have enough people who genuinely support you – people who believe in you, champion you, listen to your heart, share your secrets and celebrate your successes with you?

▶ Is there someone you would like to ask to be your mentor or ally or with whom you could share your knowledge and experience?

▶ How can you go about expanding your network so that you feel more fully supported, encouraged and nourished?

Living Our Passion

Our passion is a vital inner force that longs for expression. The things that excite and inspire us and bring us pleasure, the issues that matter most to us and the dreams that resonate deep within us are a reflection of our passion.

The more we can express our passion the more empowered we will feel to be who we really are. To do this we need to listen to our heart's calling, open ourselves up to the possibilities, cultivate our creativity and take our dreams seriously. Passionate living requires us to be willing to risk following our heart's desire and honouring our spirit within that seeks expression.

Sometimes one of the most challenging aspects of living with passion can be discovering where our passion truly lies.

It took me a while to find what I liked doing, I was so used to pleasing somebody else. I remember actually asking myself. And

I've found a whole area in my life of outdoor pursuits like kayaking and tramping and bush walks which we never did before. I've got really involved in that now. Also I love people and I'm free now to enjoy myself and play games. This is essentially me. I love the whole area of the arts, theatre, drama and I'm taking dancing lessons. By doing these things there's a fulfilment within me that actually empowers me to keep moving.

For some, expressing passion will mean doing the things we truly love. For others it will mean becoming actively involved with issues we feel strongly about. We should never underestimate the power that each of us has to make a difference. Our own unique way of making a difference is reflected in our small acts of kindness and courtesy and the support and love we give those we are close to, as well as in any issues we tackle on a larger scale.

The personal is political. Much of the social change that takes place is initiated by people who have been harmed by injustice and have decided to challenge the existing system and stand up for what they believe. These people make a valuable contribution. Through their courage and personal power our community is made a better and safer place to live.

Questions to Consider

▶ What do I love doing the most? What delights, inspires, excites me and/or warms my heart?

▶ What dreams do I hold for myself? What is my heart's desire?

▶ What issues are important to me? How can I express this passion in action?

▶ In what ways can I make my passion and dreams happen?

This chapter has offered ideas and strategies to help you to claim your personal power more fully. Each of us is capable of much more than we ever dream but without a measure of personal power we are unlikely to realise our full potential. Thus this is something well worth working towards. We each can choose how we use our power. Just as power used destructively can harm, power used wisely and well can be a tremendous force for good. From a position of personal power we can reach out and touch the lives of those around us in uplifting and inspiring ways.

CHAPTER 14

Parenting With Personal Power

Mothering is one of the most demanding tasks many of us are likely to face. It has the potential at times to reduce even the most placid, organised and good-natured among us to a dishevelled, frustrated wreck. Our offspring have the capacity to challenge us, infuriate us, hurt us, delight us and make us proud.

The parent/child relationship is not equal in terms of power. As parents we have the responsibility and right to make decisions about our children's lives. Our parental authority gives us legitimate power to guide, make rules and set limits on our child and impose discipline if necessary. With this comes the responsibility to be kind, loving and fair because our children are dependent on us. Parental power expressed with awareness, sensitivity and wisdom helps to develop a mutually respectful parent/child relationship. As our children grow we are required to increasingly loosen the reins and encourage them to make their own decisions and live their own lives. Ideally the relationship transforms into an equal one with a balance of give and take as our children reach independent adulthood.

Our own values, attitudes, beliefs, skills and the way we were parented ourselves will help to determine the way we express our power in the parent/child relationship. There are four general approaches to parenting:

▶ Permissive;
▶ Authoritarian;
▶ Passive/aggressive;
▶ Assertive.

While we will obviously vary our approach to parenting depending on our emotional resources at the time, we are likely to tend towards one style more often. Acknowledging this can be helpful.

The permissive parent has few rules and limits and often prefers to turn a blind eye to problems rather than tackling them directly. The child is indulged and allowed to have his or her way on many issues. With this style of parenting the child is often given too much freedom, choice and power and may become overly demanding and expect to have what he or she wants, regardless of the rights and needs of others. Because of the lack of guidance the child may feel insecure.

The authoritarian parent often extends strict control over the child. Rigid rules are set and the law laid down in no uncertain terms. Compliance is expected, usually without discussion or negotiation. The child has little opportunity to speak out honestly, question, assert his or her own opinion or needs, make choices or experiment. Obedience is forced by threats and punishment if necessary. This creates resentment and resistance in the child. Rather than being able to develop a sense of personal power the child is likely to become overly submissive and afraid, or imitate this model of power by also becoming bullying.

The passive/aggressive parent uses a combination of the permissive and authoritarian approach, sometimes behaving powerlessly, at other times aggressively. The parent may remain silently irritated at the child's inappropriate behaviour at times, then explode unexpectedly when a small incident pushes him or her over the edge. Because the parent's response is unpredictable and rules change unexpectedly the child is often anxious and confused. Because the child is unsure he or she may be inclined to push the boundaries and become manipulative.

Assertive parents have a high degree of personal power. They are aware of their child's rights as well as their own and are supportive of the child's budding personal power. They provide a reasonably consistent, predictable environment by setting firm, clear rules while offering choices or compromise when appropriate. Problems are dealt with honestly and fairly as they appear. While the parents may be open to negotiation they retain the right to make decisions for the child as they see fit. Assertive parents teach the child about clear boundaries, self-discipline and self-respect, trust and the rights of self and others. It is obvious the assertive approach is the most favourable in terms of creating an honest, respectful and enduring parent/child relationship.

This chapter offers suggestions and strategies for developing an assertive parenting approach and enhancing your child's sense of personal power as well as your own. It also offers ideas for defusing destructive power struggles, stopping our own hurtful behaviour towards children and dealing with children's hurtful behaviour. As you read this chapter please be gentle with yourself. Even if you realise you need to make changes it is important also to acknowledge all the countless ways you are already supporting and caring for your child.

WAYS TO INCREASE CHILDREN'S SENSE OF PERSONAL POWER

For children, gaining personal power is about developing responsibility, self-control, self-reliance and self-esteem. As parents we have enormous power to influence our children. The way we interact with our children has a huge impact on how powerful they will perceive themselves to be and how they will handle that power. If we can give our children the experience of respectful power within the vital parent/child relationship this will help them to develop their sense of positive power.

Build Children's Self-esteem

Children with high self-esteem feel good about themselves: valued, important and confident. High self-esteem goes hand in hand with a sense of personal power for children as well as adults. Children with high self-esteem are more settled in their behaviour and more resilient to the pressures of life. As daunting as it often is, our children rely on us to give them a sense of their own worth. The many gifts of approval, appreciation, support, time, encouragement, respect and commitment we give every day foster our child's self-esteem.

Give Positive Attention

Children (just like adults) respond much better to positive attention than to criticism. Giving praise not only makes the child feel valued, it is also a powerful means of encouraging appropriate behaviour. Children will seek our attention in whatever way they can. If they can't get it through positive means they will often resort to negative behaviour. When giving positive attention describe specifically the behaviour you enjoy seeing rather than using general words such as 'good'. This informs the child about the behaviours to repeat to gain positive attention. Rather than praising the achievement itself it is important to praise the effort the child makes, even if something doesn't quite work out.

Help Children to Express Feelings

It is important for children to learn to be aware of their own feelings and those of other people. We can encourage this in them by accepting and honestly talking about our own feelings and asking them about theirs. Help the child to identify confusing feelings such as doubt, anger, guilt, worry and fear and find the words to describe them. This will enable them to develop the skill of expressing their feelings verbally, rather than suppressing them or acting them out destructively. The child needs to be taught that it is okay to feel angry but it is not okay to take this out on other people. Help the child to work out a safe way to express the anger such as writing about it or drawing it.

Validate Your Children's Experience

We show children we truly respect and care for them by validating their experience. To do this we need to listen actively with an open heart, attempt to see the world through their eyes and reflect back to them our understanding of their experience. When we validate our children's experience it doesn't mean we necessarily agree with them. It means we are willing to take the time to understand where they're coming from. When we listen to their thoughts and feelings and acknowledge their point of view, even when it is different from ours, we honour them as intelligent individuals.

Aim to Be Consistent

Children need to know where they stand and what the rules and boundaries are. This helps them to be clear about what is expected and the likely consequences of non-compliance. Structure and routine help them to feel secure and settled and develop good habits. This is especially true for children with special needs or those with difficult behaviour.

Keep Children Informed

Just as we like to have a certain amount of control over our lives, so does the child. Children need to be able to make sense out of their environment and predict (to some extent) what is going to happen next. Let them know what your plans are, what to expect next and why and changes to plans, routines or decisions that have been made that affect them. At the same time be sure to keep information appropriate to the age of the child. Don't overburden the child by using him or her as a confidant.

Give Children Choices

Although we have certain rules we expect our children to follow we can often give them a choice within limits without undermining our authority. Giving a managed choice which is appropriate to the child's age and maturity helps the child to develop a sense of responsibility. For example: 'You can either spend all your pocket money now and not go to the movies or you can save it and go to the movies tomorrow.'

Encourage Children to Develop Competence

Developing a sense of being competent and having mastery over their world is vital to children's sense of self-esteem. As they grow children need to become increasingly self-reliant. They need to make choices, try out options, express opinions, make mistakes, develop their own ideas and practise self-restraint. Encourage them to do tasks appropriate to their age. Show your trust and confidence by giving responsibility and allowing them to do it their way. Don't set your expectations unrealistically high. As much as possible avoid correcting them, taking over or finishing the tasks for them.

Beware of Becoming Overprotective

Children continue to need our help and support throughout their childhood, but as they get older they also need to develop their autonomy and individuality. This calls for constant adjustment on our part. We are likely to be becoming overprotective when we find ourselves constantly worrying and feeling compelled to solve our children's problems or insisting on doing things they are quite capable of attempting for themselves. Out of our own insecurities and anxiety we may try to rigidly control our children or protect them from the consequences of their own actions. When safety is not an issue and the children are old enough to be doing certain tasks and thinking for themselves it is inappropriate to intervene persistently because of our own emotional over-involvement. By taking over unnecessarily and attempting to solve their problems we give children the message that we do not consider them competent to handle their own problems. If we are being overprotective we need to find ways to let go and trust our children to think and act for themselves. In doing this we are giving them a huge vote of confidence which will boost their sense of personal power no end.

WAYS TO INCREASE PERSONAL POWER AS A PARENT

Effective parenting is about finding a middle ground between feeling powerless and becoming overpowering: a place of personal power. Parents face the challenge of balancing parental guidance and rules for safety with allowing freedom and encouraging responsibility in the child. The complexity of our task is not helped by the fact that we are often at cross purposes with our child. Children have their own developmental need to gradually become independent and separate from us. Often they push the limits we set. Our task is to stand firm on the issues we believe are important for the child's wellbeing and safety and manage subsequent power struggles with confidence and good grace. Not an easy task!

Look after Yourself

If we don't look after ourselves adequately and take our needs seriously we can end up with very little to give our children. It's easy to become stressed and discouraged in our parenting role. Learn to notice when you are feeling tired and pressured. Even a five-minute relaxation time can make a difference to your energy and stress levels. Having a regular break away from children is not a luxury or an indulgence, it is a necessity. If possible, arrange for family or friends to give you a regular break by caring for the children. Alternatively, arrange with a friend to swap some childcare time.

Don't Be Hard on Yourself

There are no perfect parents. We all make mistakes, fall short of our aspirations and fail to handle the inevitable power struggles well. Allowing ourselves to be a 'good enough' mother is a way of taking the pressure of unrealistic expectations off ourselves. A 'good enough' mother treats her children with respect and provides relatively consistent care, love and positive attention most of the time. We are slipping into being a 'not good enough' mother when we neglect our children or overpower them with criticisms, put-downs and harsh punishment. Having acknowledged this, it is important to bring ourselves back on track as soon as possible by making positive changes.

Be Realistic in Your Expectations

Most of us want our children to behave and achieve well so we try to encourage this. However, sometimes our expectations can be so high we set ourselves and our children up for disappointment because the children simply can't live up to them. When we try to push our children beyond their capabilities resentment soon builds on both sides. We can save ourselves and our children a lot of heartache if we are realistic in the expectations we hold and learn to accept the children with the limitations they have. Become aware of the expectations you hold and consciously assess whether these are reasonable or if they are causing unnecessary friction.

Take Time to Reflect

As a parent it is important to feel reasonably in charge. This is difficult to do if we feel scattered and confused. Children often call on us to think and act quickly. It is easy to get into the habit of reacting rather than taking the time to consider our options. We are personally powerful when we feel sure about what we believe and clear about our course of action. When you are feeling pressured to make a snap decision, gain some time by saying, 'I'll think about that and let you know in . . .'

Make Your Ground Rules Explicit

As much as children resist our limits, they need them. Not only can it be frightening and unsafe to have too much freedom, it can also feel as if no-one cares. It is important to give children clear guidelines about what we expect of them so they can learn to manage their own behaviour. Be firm, clear and kind when you set boundaries. Let the child know the reasons for your request so they can make sense of it, but beware of getting drawn into arguments. As the parent you don't always have to justify why you are insisting the child follow certain rules. The way we make a request has a bearing on the outcome. Use direct eye contact and ask firmly as if you expect the child to comply. Use authority sparingly by choosing important issues to focus on. If there are several issues needing discussion it is best to focus on one or two issues at a time.

Give Clear Feedback

As we are constantly called upon to give our children feedback – both positive and negative – it is important that we find a way to do this as constructively and respectfully as possible. Focus on giving positive feedback as often as you can. A ratio of five positives to one negative has been found to be a good balance. When giving negative feedback try to be objective and calm. Keep your feedback brief. Avoid labelling the child or commenting on their capabilities or character in a derogatory way. Try using the four-part formula for assertive communication outlined in 'Become More Assertive' on p. 129.

1. Describe the unacceptable behaviour.
2. Make an 'I' statement about your feelings.
3. Say what you would like the child to do instead.
4. Say what the positive and/or negative consequence will be if the behaviour is changed or not changed.

For example:
1. 'When you hit your sister . . .
2. I feel upset and angry.
3. I'd like you to sit in that chair for the rest of this T.V. programme . . .
4. so you'll both have time to settle down. If you don't want to do that you'll have to go to your room.'

Let Them Experience Natural Consequences

There is usually a natural outcome resulting from the things we do or don't do. For example if a child doesn't remember to take his lunch to school he will be hungry and if he doesn't do his homework he will be in trouble with the teacher. It can be tempting to rescue the child from the reality of these consequences but children need to learn from their mistakes and develop a sense of responsibility for their own lives. If we continue to rescue we are teaching them that they do not need to take responsibility for their actions. If they continue to believe this the results can be disastrous.

Impose Consequences if Necessary

If there is no natural consequence for an undesirable behaviour we may need to impose one. To be effective the consequence needs to relate as closely as possible to the child's unacceptable action. For example if the child has damaged something we could insist that he or she fix or pay for the damage. We need to ensure the consequence we impose is reasonable and respectful and allows the child to maintain his or her dignity. As much as possible make sure the child knows the consequence of her behaviour ahead of time so this acts as a deterrent. The goal is to teach the child to stop and think about the possible consequence before choosing a particular course of action. We need to be prepared to be consistent in our discipline and to stand firm in the consequences we set. The challenge of this is offset by the benefits gained as the child learns to become more responsible for herself.

Take Time to Play

Just as children need time to play, so do we. Having a child offers us a wonderful opportunity to enter into the pleasure and spontaneity of our child's world. Possibilities for inexpensive fun include:

- sharing jokes and reading stories to each other;
- cooking something special together;
- having a cuddle on the sofa;
- playing a game of 'I spy';
- singing together;
- going to a funny movie;
- playing a board game;
- doing a jigsaw;
- going for a bike ride.

By spending happy, loving times together we build the relationship and give our child the message that we enjoy and appreciate them.

DEFUSING DESTRUCTIVE POWER STRUGGLES

It is only to be expected that there will be occasional power struggles with children. Mostly we find a way to weather these times and both parties emerge reasonably unscathed. Sometimes power struggles become increasingly destructive and bring out the worst in the parent and child. Both get caught in the struggle to get the upper hand, doing and saying the most wounding things to one another. At these times the parent needs to find a way to call a truce.

Take Responsibility for Defusing the Power Struggles

Although the power struggles involve both you and your child it is up to you as the adult to take the steps necessary to restore some goodwill into the wounded relationship. While you cannot control your child's responses you can control your own. When one person changes within a conflicted relationship it brings about an overall change. Whenever possible don't allow arguments to escalate into power games. Rather than fearing that the conflict is here to stay, try to see conflict as a temporary bad patch that can be worked through and resolved. There are many ways of disengaging from conflict, including:

- dropping your voice to a quiet measured tone;
- saying matter-of-factly that you don't feel like an argument;
- suggesting you both take time out;
- taking time out yourself;
- refusing to discuss contentious issues when feelings are running high;
- leaving the room or if possible going for a walk (give the time you are coming back, where you are going and why);
- inviting the child to sit down and talk about the issue quietly, either at that time or later when you are both calmer;
- acknowledging and apologising if your own behaviour has been hurtful.

Step Out of the Win/Lose Dynamic

When there are power struggles we may feel so afraid of the child getting the upper hand we will use whatever tactics we have at our disposal to 'win' the argument. We can lose sight of the damage we can do and forget that the 'loser' is likely to feel cheated and resentful and may rebel when he can. If we are becoming locked into our need to 'win' we need to stop and ask ourselves:

▶ What is the cost of my 'winning' this argument?

▶ Is it worth it?

If the price we are paying is to violate our values by becoming abusive then we need to rethink our priorities. If we are undermining our child's dignity and self-confidence in any way then we need to pull back and find another way of handling the situation. Instead of overreacting in a highly charged atmosphere take some time out to think about what is going wrong. Plan some strategies that will help to break the deadlock.

Look for Win/Win Solutions to Conflict

Win/win involves looking for a solution that both parties can live with. Finding a compromise is not a sign of weakness or giving in. Adopting a give and take attitude gives the child the message that you respect them and are willing to take their wishes into consideration. When conflict arises with older children the following strategies may be helpful:

1. Set aside some time when you are both calm to discuss the problem.

2. Agree to have two minutes each to speak uninterrupted about what the problem is for each of you and how it is affecting you. Define each of your problems clearly.

3. Work together to come up with a list of all the possible

solutions you can think of. Don't comment on or discuss the
ideas until the list is finished.

4. Choose together the solution that best meets the concerns you
    have each expressed. You need to both feel reasonably happy
    with the choice.

5. Agree to try this out for a period of time.

6. Re-evaluate the solution at a later date and modify the plan if
    necessary.

7. If tension rises during this process agree to continue the
    discussions at a later date.

Stop Using Heavy-handed Punishment

Carefully considered discipline as outlined above ('Impose
Consequences if Necessary' p. 251) has the effect of encouraging the
child's self-control. When we use punishment we attempt to impose
external control. As tempting as it may be to impose your will on your
child by using hurtful power, resist this urge. Any kind of punishment
that humiliates the child and undermines their self-worth is ultimately
going to have an adverse effect. Using destructive behaviour such as
verbal abuse, put-downs, taunts, shouting, breaking things and
hitting is harmful to the child. Power tactics invite retaliation and can
create withdrawal, resentment, bitterness and rebellion. Although
control tactics may force the child into compliance for a time it is likely
to take increasing amounts of force to achieve the same result. Then
there often comes a time when power games don't work any more. The
child begins to fight back. He or she refuses to co-operate, walks out,
becomes defiant, has angry outbursts, damages property and/or
becomes increasingly aggressive. You find yourself locked into an ugly,
escalating battle of wills that is destructive to you both. (Also see
'Stopping Hurtful Behaviour Toward Children', p. 255.)

Work to Reverse the Negative Cycle

When hurt, mistrust, disrespect and fear enter the parent/child relationship both parties may increasingly use anger and destructive behaviour to protect their vulnerabilities. The more hurt each feels, the more each wants to hurt the other. To restore the goodwill this cycle needs to be reversed. Go back to basics:

- Spend some quality time together.
- Praise and appreciate the child as much as possible.
- Ask if anything is upsetting him or her.
- Be willing to work together to resolve the conflict.
- Give clean, clear, respectful feedback about unacceptable behaviour.
- Let the child know what he or she can do to put matters right.
- Make it clear that although you do not approve of the behaviour you still love and appreciate the child.
- Have some fun time together.

STOPPING HURTFUL BEHAVIOUR TOWARDS CHILDREN

As children grow and develop they rely on us as parents to give them a sense of who they really are. Our attention and feedback, both verbal and non-verbal, is like a mirror to the child reflecting back her or his worth or lack of it. This is why we have such power to boost or damage our child's self-esteem. If we are honest, most of us occasionally misuse our power against our children. However, if this is becoming an established pattern and we know in our heart of hearts we are being disrespectful and insensitive it is time for a change. In addition to suggestions offered here, Chapter 12 'Choosing to Change' contains many further strategies.

Stop Blaming the Child

It is particularly tempting to blame our child for our hurtful behaviour:

'If you hadn't done that then I wouldn't have lost my temper.' However, we need to take responsibility for our own destructive actions. Blame keeps us stuck. The child may have behaved unacceptably but we had a choice about how we responded. By taking 100 percent responsibility for our hurtful actions we are free to put our energy into changing our behaviour. This is likely to bring about a positive change in the parent/child relationship.

Work with a Support Person

Confide in someone about your hurtful behaviour and arrange for them to support you in the changes you are making. If possible set up an agreement with them that you will phone when you are afraid you are going to behave hurtfully. Let this person know about the strategies you will use to stay safe and ask them to help you decide what to do to calm yourself down. Phone-counselling services can also offer you the opportunity to talk through your feelings and get clear on what to do.

Identify Problems Ahead of Time

Often the same old issues arise on a regular basis. It is a lot easier to think rationally and come up with solutions when we are away from the conflict. If, for example, problems always arise in the mornings spend some time reviewing the usual sequence of events, either mentally or in writing. Decide ahead of time what you can do to break the pattern. Ask yourself:

- What is causing the difficulty in this situation?
- What can I do differently here so that we can have a better outcome?

Action your ideas. Evaluate their success. If necessary modify your strategies and try again.

Recognise When You Are at Risk

High stress levels usually go hand in hand with hurtful behaviour. Practice monitoring your internal state so you notice ahead of time if you are becoming wound up. It is easy to begin unconsciously to look for someone to take your tension out on. Be particularly aware of your stress levels when you are tired, hungry, rushed, upset or under extra pressure. At these times go very gently with yourself. Make it a priority to take regular breaks.

Cool Down before Dealing with Difficult Issues

Obviously there are times when children's behaviour is out of line and we need to reprimand them in some way. If you are angry and upset your judgement is likely to be impaired and you may well react hurtfully. Whenever possible wait until you have calmed down before tackling the conflict.

If you notice you are becoming stressed take the following preventative action:

1. Stop.
2. Take your focus off the child and focus instead on yourself. Ask yourself:
   ◗ What is happening for me?
   ◗ How am I feeling?
   ◗ What do I need?
   ◗ What can I do for myself right now to bring my tension down?
3. Do it!

Take Time Out if Necessary

At the very least time out involves leaving the room that the child is in if you feel at risk of hurting your child. Ensure the child is out of harm's way first if he or she is small. If there is another adult to take over and it is possible to leave the house consider going for a walk, a run or go to visit a friend. If you can't, let the child know that you need some quiet time. Go to a private place and do some positive self-talk (see 'Use Calming Self-talk' p. 211) and relax. Also see 'Take Time Out', p. 208.

If you can't take time out do what you can to stay safe. When you are feeling stressed keep your goal of stopping hurtful behaviour at the forefront of your mind. Do whatever you need to do to support yourself in meeting this goal:

▶ Practise deep breathing.
▶ Count to 10.
▶ Remain silent rather than lashing out verbally.
▶ Sit down rather than stand over the child.
▶ Turn away or leave the room rather than becoming destructive.
▶ Calm yourself down by using the positive self talk messages listed on p. 211.
▶ Distract yourself by getting busy with something else instead.
▶ Read 'Find Ways to Soothe Yourself', p. 210 and do at least one activity from your self-soothing list.

Don't Be Afraid to Apologise

If you know you have been hurtful it is important to let the child know you are sorry. Apologising does not mean you will be seen by the child as weak. By apologising when you know you are in the wrong it is teaching the child a valuable lesson about taking responsibility for mistakes. Children tend to blame themselves for much of what happens, whether it has anything to do with them or not. Apologising relieves the child of the feelings of badness and guilt.

Seek Help if You Need To

If, for whatever reason, you find you can't implement these strategies and control your actions it is important to seek professional help. Remaining secretive about needing help will only compound the problems you are having. It may be difficult to admit to struggling with destructive behaviour but don't let this stop you. There are many options for help such as anger or stress management groups, counselling or psychotherapy. Parenting programmes usually offer valuable and constructive ideas about coping with children's challenging behaviour.

DEALING WITH CHILDREN'S HURTFUL BEHAVIOUR

Most children have their moments of using aggressive behaviour in an attempt to get their own way but when a child is persistently defying our authority, flouting our rules or attacking us verbally or physically we have a serious problem. For our child's sake as well as our own we urgently need to seek constructive ways to regain our parental authority. It can be difficult to know where to start but often the best place to start is with yourself. Work at rebuilding your personal power and confidence by following the suggestions on p. 223. Take some time to look after yourself and clarify what you need to do. Chapter 7 'Becoming More Powerful'; has many more strategies that will also help you.

Become Clear That Hurtful Behaviour Is Not Okay

When children are behaving badly it can be confusing. The issues can easily become clouded in our soul-searching and self-blame. The bottom line is that there are no excuses for destructive behaviour. This is the message you need to give the child in no uncertain terms. The stronger and more consistent the stance you take that bad behaviour is not okay, the stronger the message will be to the child that you will not tolerate it. It is amazing how when we get this clear within ourselves others often recognise the shift and begin to back off.

Stand Your Ground Consistently

Children using defiant behaviour may put enormous pressure on us to get their own way. While it may be difficult to withstand this, it is important that you do. If you frequently allow yourself to be bulldozed into changing your 'no' to 'yes' children learn that if they push hard enough they will eventually get what they want. Once learned, this pattern of pushing the limits can be very hard to break.

Hold Children Accountable

Each of us is responsible for the choices we make and the way we behave. It is vital that we are clear that when our children use hurtful behaviour they are making a choice. In the real world when we behave destructively there are certain outcomes. The sooner the child under-stands this reality the better. Don't rescue children from the conse-quences of their actions. Although we may mean well when we make excuses, bail our children out of trouble, cover up, tell lies and otherwise protect them, we are in fact depriving them of vital lessons. They need to learn from experience that there is a price to be paid for inappropriate behaviour. This can then act as a deterrent in the future.

Seek Support

If your child's behaviour is becoming increasingly out of control and aggressive don't let embarrassment and shame stop you from involving other people. Gaining support is vital. Having other people behind you can give you the boost you need to restore your parental authority. While your child may be able to overpower you he or she is unlikely to be able to accomplish this with people who are less emotionally involved. Consider contacting supportive friends and family, the school or the police. Ask them to intervene by talking to your child and for other practical assistance you need, to back you up. If your situation has escalated to the point of violence it will be especially important to involve others. It is essential that the child sees that you have back-up and learns he or she can't get away with physical abuse. Joining a Tough Love group will help you to get a perspective on what is happening and plan effective strategies that will empower you. Joining a women's Living Without Violence support group may also be helpful if you are dealing with an older child (See 'Community Resources', p. 272).

Begin to Take a Stand

If we have lost our parental authority, regaining it is likely to be a process that will take time. Start by deciding on one issue you will tackle. For example if your child has been refusing to come home for dinner you may decide to tell the child that if he or she is not home on time you will not keep dinner. Having set that limit it is important that you follow through exactly as you stated. It may sound harsh to deprive a child of dinner but this gives the message that he or she will not continue to get away with their bad behaviour. People are often surprised at how quickly taking a stand can bring about a change. If at the outset you feel apprehensive about your child's reaction arrange to have a support person with you. The important thing is to be prepared to stand firm and not back down.

Refuse to Be Drawn into Hurtful Episodes

When someone is saying hurtful things it is second nature to want to defend ourselves. This often results in an argument that may degenerate into a slanging match. Disengaging from this senseless harassment can be empowering. Make a point of refusing to be drawn into debates and arguments that are likely to leave you feeling overpowered and crushed. To set limits try saying things like:

❱ I'm not willing to talk about this right now.

❱ I refuse to discuss this with you while you are speaking to me
like this.

Deliver the message as quietly and firmly as possible, then disengage
and leave the room if necessary.

Affirm Good Behaviour

Rather than giving constant messages of disapproval try to ignore the
minor incidents of bad behaviour and constantly search for positives.
If a child is behaving badly it can be a real challenge to find things to
praise, but this is the very time we need to. When we notice okay,
ordinary behaviour and reflect this back to the child it helps the child
to connect with the best in him- or herself and gives encouragement
to keep doing the things we appreciate. When you need to give
feedback about unacceptable behaviour make it as clean, clear and
objective as possible. Let the child know that although you don't like
the destructive behaviour you do love the child.

Exercise: Assess Your Personal Power as a Parent

Maintaining a healthy balance of power in the constantly changing
parent/child relationship is enormously challenging. Most of us do the
best we can, yet despite our efforts sometimes things go wrong and this
can be extremely hard to face. Parenting difficulties strike at the very
heart of our self-esteem. To identify your strengths as a parent and
clarify where the issues (if any) lie complete the following list by
checking (✔) each statement you identify with and define to what
extent it is true for you. Place a question mark (?) beside any
statements that are partially true and leave blank those that you don't
relate to.

_____ I am seldom/sometimes/usually able to assert myself from a
position of personal power with my child.

_____ I am seldom/sometimes/usually respectful of my child's right to make mistakes, fail, have their own private thoughts or have a different point of view.

_____ I seldom/sometimes/often spend quality time with my child.

_____ When I am stressed I seldom/sometimes/often take this out on my child.

_____ I seldom/sometimes/usually set clear rules and boundaries for my child.

_____ I am inclined to rescue my child from the consequences of her/his actions.

_____ I am seldom/sometimes/usually sensitive to my child's feelings.

_____ I am seldom/sometimes/often unpredictable in the way I respond to my child.

_____ I am inclined to overprotect my child because I feel anxious.

_____ I am seldom/sometimes/often inclined to be overbearing.

_____ I usually give my child more positive than negative feedback.

_____ I am inclined to give in to pressure from my child and change my 'no' to 'yes'.

_____ I seldom/sometimes/often feel powerless and/or afraid of my child.

_____ I seldom/sometimes/often expect too much of my child and become angry when he/she doesn't measure up.

_____ When my child disagrees with me I seldom/sometimes/often become unreasonable and overpowering.

_____ I seldom/sometimes/often become intolerant or impatient or use put-downs, ridicule, sarcasm or other power games.

_____ When power struggles erupt I sometimes/often resort to power-over tactics in order to 'win'.

_____ I tend to be erratic in my use of carefully thought out discipline.

_____ I seldom/sometimes/often use heavy-handed punishment
like put-downs, verbal abuse or hitting.

_____ I am sometimes/often afraid I am going to hurt my child
physically.

Honestly completing this checklist may have been a sobering
experience. If you have identified areas of concern it will be important
to keep a perspective on this. Because of the demanding nature of
bringing up children there will always be room for improvement for
most of us. It is vital to affirm yourself for all the efforts you are
making. Most of us will have areas of strength as well as particularly
challenging areas. If we are off-track with certain aspects of our
parenting it is not about beating ourselves up – it is about acknowledging this and learning to do things differently.

If you are feeling distressed or overwhelmed right now, share your
feelings with your support person or write about them in your journal.
If you need to make changes take the time to work out some new
strategies with your support person. It can be comforting to remember
that bringing up children is a work in progress. Despite mistakes we
have made it is possible to change. If we honestly acknowledge where
we are going wrong and constantly renew our efforts to bring
ourselves back on track, results can often be seen surprisingly quickly.
One woman expressed her parenting goal this way:

*The underlying catalyst for change is to try and give my children
as little baggage as possible to walk away from this house with. I
can't undo what has happened but I can give them new tools. I can
help build their self-esteem and self-worth, talk to them about
honesty and self-love and teach them things so they know that as
adults they're responsible for their own life and the choices they
make.*

CHAPTER 15

Final Words

These final words about personal power are spoken by the women who so generously shared their stories in order that this book could be written. May their courage and wisdom inspire you and touch your heart as they have ours.

At times growth has been painful, and at times growth has been sweet, but it has always been fulfilling and very releasing. Other women I've talked to who are on the journey of growth have all agreed that once they started, it was like a thirst. They wanted to keep going. And regardless of how rocky it may get at any given time they actually don't want to step back from it because there is relief that comes with it. There's a freedom, and self-ownership which if you haven't had, you can't believe.

I have always been afraid of my power. At the heart of everything has been a running away from my power because I saw power so abused. I wanted to learn wisdom before I took power. I've done that by seeing everything as an opportunity to learn about myself, about humanity, about what the truth of life is. To learn about deeper questions in life as though I'm a student. My mission has been to find the truth, to find God, to find love – basically to find my essence.

I believe all difficulties can be worked through because we are powerful beings, all of us. I think that life gives you situations, and people sometimes appear to be enemies, but these are the difficulties by which the heart is awakened. From my experience I would say, if the action doesn't seem wholesome then move away from it.

The biggest thing for me has been learning to forgive myself and to see myself as being capable of change. And understanding that what happened to me was not my fault. I was originally abused by someone who was very important to me. That left me vulnerable to a whole series of other abuses. Until I began to heal I actually wasn't capable of making proper judgements, I didn't have the skills to cope with situations, and people took advantage of that.

When I found who I really am I found a new power within myself that I never knew was there. It is a power to be real, to be that very person that I need to be. And that is the most freeing thing. I don't have to pretend any more.

I didn't know for most of my life that I was able to make choices and that I could change my choices again if they weren't working. Realising that has been really freeing. When I felt powerless I tried to claim the power by being destructive. Now I have my self-worth and personal power and I know what behaviour is acceptable. I have more of an insight into how things are, and it has become true that I treat others how I want to be treated.

It has been important for me to learn to look at the full picture, not just to see things at a personal level and think I'm the only one with problems. There's been a growth of my own understanding through reading a lot of feminist literature and realising that women do live in a very shitty system that is stacked against them in a lot of ways. There are many women who are articulate, intelligent, gentle, good people who are put down because they try to get heard. Why should women have to fight to be heard? It's so unjust at times. I'd like women to become powerful and to take their rightful, equal position in society.

I've discovered that lots of tiny little steps will get me where I want to go. I don't have to do it all at once. And it's okay for me to try and fail. What I've been through doesn't make me incapable, it just means I have more stuff to deal with than most people. It also makes me very aware of what other people are going through, so there are advantages. I'm learning to accept my own imperfections. I'm not going to always get it right. It has taken 38 years to get to this point. It's not going to come right in 38 weeks. It's going to take a while. I'm learning the best way for me to get through is to be really, really honest and to learn some techniques to make my family safe and myself safe during the process.

Things began to change after I started to think, 'My life is really unsatisfactory. Who am I? Where does true empowerment come from?' I'm still working on finding that out. So far I've found that it comes from facing life, standing on my own two feet, not pulling the wool over my eyes, owning up to my difficulties and frailties as a human being – my anger or the things that I might do as a form of control or to manipulate someone. Just being more self-aware has helped.

I've learnt there's someone out there who will offer the door of change. You can walk through it if you choose to, you really can. And when you've walked through the door and made changes, then you can open that door for someone else, through the knowledge you have. You share with others and then they can pass it on, and pass it on and pass it on. I think that in the long term that's where our community and people can become healthier.

As I've become more aware of my spiritual self and become more connected to it I feel so much more whole. When I find myself getting into my old scattered, anxious state I stop and focus within and consciously bring my energy back into my body and open up to God and let peace and power fill me. It's amazing how that calms me. I'm learning more and more that I don't have to go it alone. When the going gets tough I get the strength to keep going from this limitless source. That support and love and power is there for me constantly: I just have to remember to call on it and to open up to receive it.

The funniest thing I've discovered since I've changed is that I'm the most sensitive, loving, caring person and I've gained so much more being like that. Before I wasn't in touch with the sensitive part of myself. I just used to be so horrible to people. Now I've gained more of the lovely, beautiful things in my life.

It's like I feel I've been carrying this heavy weight around for years but now I feel a lot more pleasure than I ever used to. I think the most difficult thing is to lighten up. It's been a real heavy scene. Now I'm building my self-worth so that I can go out into the world with joy and spread that joy. I think the most important gift you can give is your joy, your lightness, your happiness. That's the next stage for me. To be able to skip through the fields, to laugh and sing and lighten up, to toss off the load. I don't have to carry it any more.

I know who I am now. I feel like I have a spirit. Before it was like I was lost. It was like my spirit was apart from me, disconnected, just waiting for me to pick it up. I feel now I have an identity, I know who I am and what I'm here for. It's like my spirit now belongs to me.

Know Your Rights

Where power games are being played someone's rights are usually being violated, but we may fail to recognise this violation, much less challenge it. Considering that traditionally women had few rights it is hardly surprising that at times we are confused about the behaviours we are entitled to expect from other people. The following list of rights can be used as a guide. Others are also entitled to expect these same behaviours from us.

- ▶ I am entitled to be treated with respect and dignity, to be listened to and taken seriously.
- ▶ I am entitled to make my own decisions and take responsibility for the outcome.
- ▶ I am entitled to have and to express my own opinions, ideas and values.
- ▶ I am entitled to say no without justifying myself and feeling guilty.
- ▶ I am entitled to express my feelings – including anger.
- ▶ I am entitled to personal space and privacy.
- ▶ I am entitled to choose who I spend time with.

- I am entitled to change my mind, not know things, fail and make mistakes.
- I am entitled to ask for or refuse help.
- I am entitled to state my needs, ask others to meet them or meet them myself.
- I am entitled to have a life that is safe, free, happy and peaceful.

Questions to Consider

- Do you feel entitled to claim each of these rights for yourself?
- Which of these rights are you finding it difficult to claim?
- What are you afraid might happen if you were to assert your rights more fully?
- Are you stepping on anybody else's rights?
- What changes (if any) would you like to make?

Community Resources

There are many organisations that offer support, information and assistance. The following list covers some of them. If these organisations cannot offer you the kind of support you need, ask them to recommend another that may be suitable.

Counselling and therapy

Alcoholics Anonymous
Tel 0845 769 7555

Asian Family Counselling Service
76 Church Road, London W7 1LB
Tel 020 8567 5616

British Association of Counselling
1 Regents Place, Rugby, Warks
Tel 01788 550 899

British Association of Psychotherapists
37 Mapesbury Road, London NW2 4HJ
Tel 020 8452 9823

ChildLine
Tel 0800 1111

Jewish Marriage Counselling
23 Ravenhurst Avenue, London NW4 4EE
Tel 020 8203 6311/Crisis line 0345 581 999
Offer face-to-face counselling in Manchester and three centres in London.

Mind
Headquarters, Granta House, 15–19 Broadway, Stratford, London E15 4BQ
Tel 020 8519 2122
Mental health information, advice and support groups. Check your phone directory for local services.

National Workplace Bullying Service
Tel 01235 834548

Parentline
Tel 01702 559900
For parents under stress.

Rape Crisis Centres
Rape crisis groups have well-trained people who offer support and counselling to survivors of sexual abuse and rape. See your phone directory for your local service.

Relate
Herbert Gray College, Little Church Street, Rugby, Warks CV21 3AP
Tel 01788 573241
Couples counselling.

Samaritans
Tel 0845 790 9090 (24-hour phone counselling service)/
(textphone) 0845 790 9192
Or check your phone directory for your local service.

SeniorLine
Tel 0808 800 6565/(textphone) 0800 269626

Women's Therapy Centre
10 Manor Gardens, London N7 6JS
Tel 020 7263 6200

Legal advice and mediation

Children's Legal Centre
Tel 01206 873 820

Citizens Advice Bureaux
The Citizens Advice Bureaux are excellent sources of information about local social service agencies, support groups, courses, legal rights, housing, welfare and health issues. The CAB also offer a free legal advice service in many areas (by appointment) and a free budgeting service. Check your phone directory for your local CAB's phone number.

Epoch
77 Holloway Road, London N7 8JZ
Tel 020 7700 0627
Campaigns against physical punishment and advises on positive child rearing.

National Council for One Parent Families
255 Kentish Town Road, London NW5 2LX
Tel 0800 018 5026
info@oneparentfamilies.org.uk

National Family Mediation
9 Tavistock Place, London WC1H 9SN

Tel 020 7383 5993
Will put you in touch with an affiliated family mediation service near you.

Solicitors Family Law Association
PO Box 302, Orpington, Kent BR6 8QX
Tel 01689 850227
Refer you to a solicitor specialising in dealing with family law.

Release
388 Old Street, London EC1V 9LT
Tel 020 7729 9904
Drugs and legal helpline.

Rights of Women
52–54 Featherstone Street, London EC1Y 8RT
Tel 020 7251 6577
Legal advice for women.

Women's Aid

A network offering safe, confidential accommodation to women who are
leaving an abusive relationship, along with their children. They provide
support, information and practical assistance.

Women's Aid Federation England
Tel 0845 702 3468

Northern Ireland Women's Aid
Tel 0801 2322 49041

Scottish Women's Aid
Tel 0131 475 2372

Welsh Women's Aid, Aberystwyth
Tel 01970 612748

Welsh Women's Aid, Cardiff
Tel 02920 390874

Welsh Women's Aid, Rhyl
Tel 01745 334767

Employment

Commission for Racial Equality
Elliot House, Allington Street, London SW1E 5EH
Tel 020 7828 7022

Criminal Injuries Compensation Board
Tel 020 7936 3476

Trade Union Congress
Congress House, Great Russell Street, London WC1B 3LS
Tel 020 7636 4030
Information about trade unions.

INDEX

Established in 1978, The Women's Press publishes
high-quality fiction and non-fiction from outstanding
women writers worldwide. Our list spans literary fiction,
crime thrillers, biography and autobiography, health,
women's studies, literary criticism, mind body spirit, the
arts and the Livewire Books series for young women.
Our bestselling annual *Women Artists Diary* features the
best in contemporary women's art.

The Women's Press also runs a book club through
which members can buy, every quarter, the best fiction
and non-fiction from a wide range of British publishing
houses, mostly in paperback, always at discount.

To receive our latest catalogue, or for information on
The Women's Press Book Club, send a large SAE to:

The Sales Department
The Women's Press Ltd
34 Great Sutton Street London EC1V 0LQ
Tel: 020 7251 3007 Fax: 020 7608 1938
www.the-womens-press.com

Kay Douglas
Invisible Wounds
A Self-Help Guide for Women in Destructive Relationships

All couples have power struggles and disagreements at times, but there is a difference between a relationship with the usual ups and downs and one that constitutes emotional abuse. In this practical, accessible and supportive book, Kay Douglas draws on the first-hand accounts of over 50 women – as well as her own personal experience – to demonstrate how to recognise, resolve and recover from a destructive relationship. With advice on how to work out what is *really* happening within a relationship; how to clarify needs and feelings; deal with an abusive partner; get the support we need; cope with the effects on children; regain our power in the relationship or decide to leave it; and how to heal, this is an essential book for all women who have, or have had, partners who are emotionally abusive.

Self-help £8.99
ISBN 0 7043 4450 5

Kathy Nairne and Gerrilyn Smith
Dealing with Depression

Second Edition – Fully revised and updated

Why do so many women suffer from depression? How can we defend ourselves against this common problem and get out of what can quickly become a vicious circle?

Kathy Nairne and Gerrilyn Smith, both clinical psychologists, draw on their extensive professional experience together with the experiences of a wide range of women sufferers to offer this down-to-earth and comprehensive guide. From identifying the causes of depression to understanding the many forms it can take, from different ways of coping and recovering to evaluating the help available, here is an essential handbook for anyone who has experienced depression, either in themselves or others.

'A straightforward, practical guide . . . it explores its subject in depth' *Company*

'I can thoroughly recommend this practical, sympathetic and non-patronising book'
London Newspaper Group

Health/Self-help £6.99
ISBN 0 7043 4443 2

Belinda Grant Viagas
Stress
Restoring Balance to Our Lives

Stress can cause illness, ruin relationships and result in long-term health problems. At worst, it is a killer. But it can also be a positive, motivating, even life-saving force. In this eye-opening book Belinda Grant Viagas examines some of the specific pressures that women encounter and builds up a resource of practical methods to deal with stress in its many guises, and restore harmony to our lives. She looks at how to:

- recognise the physical and psychological signs of stress
- identify just how much or how little stress you need
- introduce relaxation techniques into your daily regime
- devise long-term coping strategies
- prepare 'quick fix' stress-busters
- identify the foods that stress you out
- explore the roots of stress
- develop positive self-awareness

With a combination of short-term and long-term strategies, this book will help you define your own optimum stress levels for maintaining efficiency, enthusiasm and drive.

Health/Self-help
ISBN: 0 7043 4633 8

Delcia McNeil
Bodywork Therapies for Women
A Guide

This informative guide examines the numerous bodywork
therapies available, with particular focus on their relevance
to women's physical and emotional health.

Including:

- Massage, Osteopathy
- Hypnotherapy, Rebirthing
- Traditional Chinese Medicine, Acupuncture
- Rolfing, Alexander Technique, Pilates
- Metaphysical Healing
- Bioenergetics, Gestalt
- Trager® Approach, Zero Balancing
- Yoga, Tai Chi and more.

Delcia McNeil examines each therapy in turn, outlining which
conditions it will help alleviate and explaining its theoretical
background and philosophy. She also clarifies what to expect at
each bodywork session and provides advice on how to find a
practitioner as well as suggesting self-help techniques to try at
home.

Above all, McNeil advocates a holistic approach to health and
the body – highlighting the effectiveness of focused touch, non-
invasive treatments, sensitivity and intuition.

Health/Mind, Body, Spirit £8.99
ISBN: 0 7043 4569 2

Stephanie Dowrick
Intimacy and Solitude
Balancing Closeness and Independence

Why is it that when we are in intimate relationships, we may often feel dissatisfied, inadequate and claustrophobic? But then, once we are on our own, we get lonely and have difficulties enjoying solitude? In this internationally bestselling book, Stephanie Dowrick draws on a wide range of personal experiences, and on psychotherapy's most useful insights, to show how success in intimacy depends on success in solitude – and vice versa.

Whether experiencing solitude through choice or through circumstance, *Intimacy and Solitude* enables us to discover our own unique inner world – and offers real possibilities for lasting, positive change.

'Sympathetically, and with a rare clarity, it offers penetrating insights into some of the most basic paradoxes of human relationships' *Guardian*

'Essential reading . . . A penetrating, thoroughly researched, thoughtful and thought-provoking analysis. Don't stay home on your own without it'
Mary Scott, *Everywoman*

Self-help/Therapy/Sexual Politics £7.99
ISBN 0 7043 4308 8